THE AI HANDBOOK
— FOR SALES —
PROFESSIONALS

A Practical, Tactical Guide for Sellers, Managers,
and Executives to Reclaim Their Time
and Expand Their Humanity

JD Miller, PhD

The AI Handbook for Sales Professionals
A Practical, Tactical Guide for Sellers, Managers, and Executives to Reclaim Their Time and Expand Their Humanity

ISBN: 979-8-89576-195-3 (Paperback)
ISBN: 979-8-89576-196-0 (Hardcover)
ISBN: 979-8-89576-197-7 (eBook)

Author Photo Credit: Organic Headshots
Editing: Mary Rembert

*"The world only spins forward. We will be citizens.
The time has come."*

—Tony Kushner, *Angels in America*

TABLE OF CONTENTS

INTRODUCTION

The convocation speaker's words rang clearly. "When you graduate in four years, the vast majority of you will go to work in jobs that have not yet been invented."

It was 1993, and my freshman class at the University of Illinois was among the first to receive email addresses as a standard part of our enrollment.

Urbana-Champaign was one of six supercomputing centers that formed the "backbone" of the early internet, with high-speed connections linking us to Cornell and Princeton on the East Coast, the University of California, San Diego, on the west, and a few points in between.

Across campus, a number of computer labs were available to students, who could tap directly into the internet using NCSA Mosaic. It was the first web browser that allowed access to images inline with text in a point-and-click interface, and one of its UIUC-based developers— Marc Andreessen—would later team up with Silicon Graphics' founder Jim Clark to develop its commercial successor, Netscape Navigator.

The speaker's prediction rang true. When I left campus a few years later, I had an advanced degree in social networking and internet-based communication, and I took a first job building an intranet that would connect the 3,000 employees of a global company to a single information and communication base.

My classmates and I entered the workforce as digital natives—browsing the web and emailing one another as naturally and unthinkingly as our more senior colleagues typed memos to fax to one another.

The conversations around our offices were full of questions. What does this "World Wide Web" really mean for our business? Is it a fad? Do I have to use it? Will it put me out of a job?

The media joined in. *Newsweek* assured readers that "no online database will replace your daily newspaper," even as the headlines printed out and dropped in front of millions of doors each morning predicted that telecommuting would soon be available to a majority of workers, delivery of perishable groceries could never be mediated by a website, and any number of other ideas that were soon proven false.

Thirty years later, we're having many of the same conversations about a different technological advancement: generative AI.

Early-adopting business leaders and AI boosters are excited about the potential for AI to enhance productivity, bring new products to market faster, and deliver unparalleled, personalized customer experiences.

On the other hand, naysayers point to the tendency of AI to hallucinate, arrive at incorrect results on basic math questions, and perpetuate hidden biases from their training data as reasons it will never become part of the mainstream.

Like the internet of the late 90s, I believe the truth lies somewhere in the middle.

When I worked with a major airline to build the first web-based airport check-in kiosks, many were concerned about how many customer service agents would lose their jobs. While it's true today that there is less need for traditional customer service agents to help flyers buy airline tickets over the phone, the ease of self-service has contributed to a massive increase in flight volumes. More than five times as many air passengers are carried globally today as in 1990, increasing the demand for newer, different sorts of airline-related jobs than before.

Early in my management career, I was taught to delegate work to the lowest-cost resource who could accomplish the job successfully. It was advice from a seller who had risen through the ranks to manage a team—instructing me to let go of the day-to-day tactics of managing every deal, teaching my team members to do that effectively so I could spend my time doing higher-level work on more strategic tasks.

Today, AI tools enable us to delegate much more work, and the lowest-cost resource we can send it to is now a computer algorithm, rather than an entry-level worker.

My leadership career has also been informed by my training as a social scientist, which tells me that some skills—particularly those related to interpersonal trust and relationship-building—can only be successfully accomplished by a living, breathing human being.

While I know I'm not smart enough to make precise predictions about exactly how AI will transform our work and personal lives, I am confident it will have a seismic impact.

I think about the web skeptics from years ago who now access it multiple times a day from the phones in their pockets, and I know we can't pretend AI technologies won't seriously change our professional and personal lives. But I'm just as sure that those advances will still leave us with jobs that value people with great social and communication skills.

That's why I'm writing this book.

As a career sales leader who has lived through one revolution, I'm seeing a familiar pattern—and I want to help everyone thrive at this new intersection of business, technology, and humanity.

As an operating advisor and sales-focused board member in private equity, I have front-row access to the work of dozens of companies as they simultaneously experiment with various AI tools in their businesses. To keep my own knowledge, skills, and advice relevant to them, I conducted a wide-ranging survey of over 140 AI tools to understand what they do, where there's been great success (and great disappointments!), and what the future might look like.

I share my findings here as a practical, tactical roadmap for other sales professionals to use in navigating the AI revolution. The book is for quota-carrying sellers, frontline managers, chief revenue officers, boards, and executive teams who feel the shifting ground and want to be on top when everything settles.

In the following chapters, I'll break down exactly what AI is, explore current applications for all levels of sales professionals, look at how to get started today, consider the ethical implications, and think a bit about where all of this might be heading.

Throughout, I've provided examples of AI use cases that are already in use, marketed, or contemplated by a variety of technology vendors. I do so knowing that—like the tech landscape of the late 90s—this is a rapidly growing marketplace. Feature sets will become commoditized, new capabilities will arise, new players will enter the market, some will go out of business, others will consolidate, and what seems like a competitive differentiator or functionality gap today may no longer be the case tomorrow.

Indeed, just as this book heads to press, two key vendors—Clari and Salesloft—announced their merger, illustrating how quickly the landscape can shift as vendors try to offer even more comprehensive, value-added solutions.

Steve Cox, the CEO of the combined company, illustrated this ambition in his statement that "by bringing together two category leaders, we'll transform how companies run revenue in the AI era … we'll be accelerating AI innovation for our customers—doubling our

R&D investment to build the Predictive Revenue System and create a revenue flywheel that drives productivity and growth."[1]

Where I've described the functionality of specific products, then, it's less important to think of them as a specific capability offered by a specific vendor—and more as an example of what the class of AI technologies can do for the modern sales professional, which you can then use as a jumping off point of use cases to do your own vendor research and selection.

This book isn't about hyping AI—or about naysaying. It's about having a handbook to explore where AI can help you win in an ever-evolving world.

---

[1] Steve Cox, "Clari and Salesloft Complete Merger, Appoint Steve Cox as CEO to Build First Predictive Revenue System," Clari and Salesloft Complete Merger, Appoint Steve Cox as CEO to Build First Predictive Revenue System, accessed January 22, 2026, https://www.salesloft.com/company/newsroom/clari-salesloft-merger.

DEMYSTIFYING AI

Before jumping into tactical guidance on applying AI to sales, it's helpful to get a basic grounding in what it is.

The release of ChatGPT in November 2022 threw a public spotlight on AI—and to many, it seemed like a magical genie in a bottle was suddenly unleashed on the other side of a social media prompt.

Yet as early as 1948, Alan Turing was thinking about intelligent machines that could "play a not very bad game of chess." His 1950 paper, "Computing Machinery and Intelligence," proposed that computers would pass a test of their ability to exhibit intelligent behavior if a human could not reliably tell the difference between another human and a machine in a transcript of a conversation between the two.

From these earliest days, pattern recognition has been at the core of AI technologies, and as computing power has intensified, these tools have been able to handle larger datasets and make more complex predictions from them.

In the early 80s, word processing programs could be prompted to comb through every word in a text and flag anything the user had mistyped ("recieve," for example) that wasn't listed in a preapproved dictionary of correctly spelled words. Users had to start this search proactively, and it often took a few minutes to flag each misspelled word in their document. It was a rules-based system ("if this word is not on the list, then highlight it in red"), and it was typical of the first generation of symbolic AI tools (or good old-fashioned AI—GOFAI) that sought to capture and manipulate human intelligence into an ever-increasing, ever-more-complex rulebook for operation.

A few years later, processing power increased, and "recieve" could not only be flagged as wrong, but "receive" might be suggested as the English word with the closest typographical similarity to the misspelled one, and therefore the word that is statistically most likely to be what the writer intended.

Another revolution in processing power, and this thinking could be done in real time, significantly improving the user experience. Suddenly, a user who started to type "rec ..." was offered auto-suggested options of "receive," "recent," and "reception," as real-time completions of their thoughts as they typed.

A similar ability to identify patterns and make predictions based on past observations has been powering other common AI experiences in our lives—from recommending books to read or movies to watch based on the last one purchased, identifying potentially fraudulent credit card transactions that don't fit the pattern of previous purchases, to predicting traffic delays on a given highway at a particular time of day.

Here, the AI tools aren't simply following a set of predetermined rules—they're constantly refining their algorithms based on an ever-expanding volume of user-generated data (of viewing patterns, purchases, or car speeds)—in a new style of AI called "machine learning."

The introduction of ChatGPT, then, wasn't a new fundamental concept in AI. It was a change in scale.

The technological underpinning of ChatGPT was increased computing power (enabled by advances in computer chip technology from companies like NVIDIA), which allowed faster and faster pattern analysis on bigger and bigger datasets with ever-more-complex relationships.

Algorithms were already predicting that users who began sentences with "receive" might be completing their sentence with "a free gift with purchase," and this burst in computing power spread the scope of prediction much wider.

No longer was the technology consulting a few hundred pages of dictionary words to look for patterns between individual letters—it was pulling from a few hundred million pages of text to identify which words come next … and eight paragraphs later … and 12 pages before … and all sorts of permutations and relationships between the other words in between—to generate paragraphs and pages of new content in your conversation. And while the first word processing spellcheckers took a few minutes to run, all of these generative AI calculations could happen in a matter of seconds.

A similar process allowed AI image generation (and later, video generation) to gain widespread traction … looking at how individual pixels and groups of pixels relate to one another in an ever-expanding library of images that are known to be of "a birthday cake," "a cute kitten," or "the Taj Mahal."

While these applications have become widely accessible and adopted by lots of people in a short time for very broad tasks, they join a number of other tools designed for specific purposes.

When we look at the process of identifying regularities, recurring structures, and meaningful trends within datasets—as well as their outliers—we find applications in medicine (like using AI to flag chest X-rays that might indicate early signs of cancer), automotive design (where AI is used to alert drivers with beeps or vibrations when it detects lane dividers or road obstructions within a specific field of vision), or search and rescue operations (where AI tools scan drone footage of vast, remote areas for anomalies in the landscape that might be a lost person).

The breadth of these applications seems to allow us to put an AI label on just about everything in common culture. NASA's definition—which broadly defines AI as "any artificial system that can perform tasks under unpredictable circumstances without significant human oversight, learn from experience, or solve tasks requiring human-like perception, cognition, and communication"—fits very well.

In writing this book, I used a similarly broad definition of AI to explore as many tools and processes as practical for the modern sales professional.

HOW IS AI DEPLOYED?

As AI tools are built for specific purposes (to create a sales forecast or suggest the best case study to offer up in response to a customer objection), they typically follow a four-step workflow:

1. **Data Collection:** A large dataset relevant to the task is collected. Just as a spam filter relies on thousands of emails to make its classifications, a sales tool may look to transcripts of call recordings or CRM databases full of information about won and lost opportunities to feed its analysis.

2. **Feature Extraction:** This step involves identifying the most important characteristics (or "features") of the data for the model to analyze. In early machine learning, engineers typically had to manually define these features. But today, an exciting hallmark of AI is its ability to identify important, unexpected characteristics on its own.

   Consider Gong's research, which found that sellers are 8% more likely to win deals when their prospect curses on the call and the seller follows suit. This illustrates the power of "deep learning"—the system's ability to automatically detect highly complex, abstract patterns (in this case, the likely indication that the seller has developed a deep rapport and trust with their prospect) that a human might never think to label as an important feature of their data.

3. **Model Training:** The AI engine is "trained" on the dataset, iteratively adjusting its parameters to learn the statistical relationship between the input features and the desired result. This may take a "supervised" learning form, where humans are involved in labeling data (as "spam," for example, or as "a good answer to the customer's question").

   An "unsupervised" approach may also be taken, in which the model is given unlabeled data and must find hidden structures on its own (for example, segmenting customers or buyers into different categories or personas based on their purchasing behavior without being told what those categories should be).

   Often, a combination of both is used—the system begins with an unsupervised learning approach, and its work is then checked by humans with real-world expertise until the model has been refined into a highly effective one.

4. **Prediction or Classification:** Once trained, the model can be given new, unseen data and use the patterns it's learned to make a prediction or assign a classification to new scenarios (a new customer request through an online chat form, for example). This is the phase where the AI tool is "in production" for a business purpose.

WHAT ARE ITS LIMITATIONS?

Breakthroughs in AI offer a lot of promise—and their ability to produce text that passes the "Turing Test" of 1950 has a lot of folks imagining all sorts of roles for AI at their companies in the future. It's important, though, to remember that the ways these tools work bake in fundamental limitations that are often easy to overlook in our enthusiasm for novel experiences.

AI tools are well-suited to tasks involving identifying and categorizing differences among data points. They're great at answering questions like "What is this?" or discriminating between whether a data point belongs in "category A" or "category B."

For sellers, finding answers to discriminative questions like "Is this a prospect with a high propensity to buy?" or "Does this conversation suggest that this person has decision-making power or not?" is a natural fit for AI tools.

AI tools are also good fits for generative tasks. Once it has learned the underlying pattern and the deep underlying structure of a dataset, an AI tool can generate new original data samples that are statistically similar to the data it was trained on.

It can summarize important points in a legal contract, produce answers to questions typically found in RFPs, or prompt sellers with the best next steps to take in deals based on what other activities led to wins in prior situations—and it's able to do this well because of its ability to send its work product to a discriminating task that can categorize various suggestions as more like the "good" or the "bad" examples it's been trained on.

At the same time, AI is not yet great at carrying context over long time periods. Some tools are only immediately reactive to this moment's input (Shazam, for example, can identify that you're listening to the "Winter" movement of Vivaldi's Four Seasons, but when doing so, it doesn't remember or care that it just identified the "Spring" movement a few minutes earlier).

Other tools may operate with limited memory of interactions, constantly interpreting recent ones (like a customer service chatbot that remembers your name and account number for the duration of your call but asks for them again the next time you contact support).

Even when information carries over from one interaction to another, though, these systems don't have a persistent, conscious "memory" in the same way that human beings do—and, indeed, tend to "lose the plot" in extended conversations with users.

Similarly, today's AI lacks a "theory of mind" that understands that humans have their own beliefs, desires, intentions, and emotions that will affect their behavior.

If you've ever called a utility company to report a service outage and been offered only the option to "press one to make a payment" by an automated voice that continues to offer this cheery option even after you've screamed and sworn at it that you want something different, you have found this limitation in AI.

Increasingly, it feels like more sophisticated AI tools have developed personalities, and many people develop parasocial relationships with AI bots that they consider their "friend" or "therapist." However, it's important to remember that while AI can learn to simulate empathy and emotion by offering canned responses like "you're welcome" when it hears "thank you" or "I'm sorry, I didn't catch that" to unexpected user prompts, today's AI systems do not genuinely understand the underlying emotions of their users.

In this vein, science fiction writers imagine a world where an AI system possesses its own consciousness—one that not only understands the emotions of others but also has its own self-aware motivations and feelings. They make great stories, but these tools do not exist today.

Generative AI tools may indeed tell you that "they're having a great day," or "are disappointed that it's going to rain this afternoon," but they're doing so because they've learned those are the words that are most frequently used responses to the weather data they've been trained on—nothing more.

Because AI tools are most limited in these essentially human, empathetic communication processes, and because these skills are at the core of sales processes, I'm confident that AI will not eliminate the sales profession.

Like the customer service agents from the 1990s airlines, though, I do believe that sellers need to evolve—and those who learn to delegate repetitive, data-driven tasks to AI while using the results to be even more impactful with innately "human" tasks like empathy, trust-building, and relationship development will be the high performers of the future.

At the same time, sellers who don't adapt risk becoming the 1990s encyclopedia salesmen: a relic whose primary asset—knowing the facts—was instantly devalued when information became a universal commodity.

To stay relevant through the shift, sales professionals can't just do their old jobs faster—they need to evolve into AI-enabled professionals who use technology to amplify their most uniquely human strengths—empathy, trust, and strategic judgment.

GETTING READY FOR AI

If we accept that AI is taking the same trajectory as web technologies did at the turn of the century, it is not something we should ignore or expect to go away. For modern businesses (and their sales professionals), AI usage is a strategic imperative for competitive survival and growth.

AI adoption is not just another tool to incorporate into the usual way of doing things—it's the lever for a fundamental business transformation, and navigating this shift is a mandate for every employee.

The measurable, significant gains that early adopters have realized explain why. A 2024 Salesforce report found that salespeople spend only 28% of their time actually selling.[2] Using AI tools to automate tasks like data entry and scheduling can reclaim a lot of the time spent on this sort of "administrivia"—creating more opportunities for customer interaction, relationship building, and strategic selling.

Moreover, a Bain & Company report suggests that some organizations that have used AI to inform their execution at every stage of the sales pipeline—from lead generation to closing—have improved their win rates by as much as 30%.[3]

---

[2] "State of Sales Report," Salesforce, accessed February 10, 2026, https://www.salesforce.com/sales/state-of-sales/.

[3] Ann Bosche et al., "Ai Is Transforming Productivity, but Sales Remains a New Frontier," Bain, December 17, 2025, https://www.bain.com/insights/ai-transforming-productivity-sales-remains-new-frontier-technology-report-2025/.

Results like these don't come simply by plugging in a new piece of technology, though. Successful AI deployments require a clear strategy, a strong data foundation, and an organizational culture that is open to change—and each of these is driven by the leadership team. The chief revenue officer, of course, needs to be a key sponsor of AI solutions for the GTM (go-to-market) org, but they also need to collaborate closely with the leaders of HR, IT, finance, and marketing to make these projects a success.

I've found it helpful to have an AI Readiness Maturity Model to guide an organization's progress with AI tools. The model provides a structured framework to assess an organization's current capabilities, establish realistic short- and long-term goals, and proactively manage risks that have derailed other tech deployments.

My model includes three levels of sophistication, ranging from some early, tentative experiments, through a more advanced stage, and ultimately a fully AI-enabled way of working.

This chart helps assess your AI readiness and maturity across six dimensions. While it's possible that you'd score your own organization's maturity as low/level 1 across all the dimensions if you're just starting out, I suspect you're more likely to find some areas where you're already well advanced, and others where you've got room to grow.

Assessment Dimension	Level 1: Foundational (Experiment & Prepare)	Level 2: Advanced (Scale & Routinize)	Level 3: AI-Enabled (Transform & Innovate)
Strategic Vision & Business Alignment	The organization views AI as a "nice to have" productivity tool, and may be exploring pockets of ad hoc experimentation—particularly on specific pain points that yield quick wins (e.g., automatic call transcripts and meeting summaries that identify critical next steps).	The organization views AI as a competitive advantage. There are strategic projects underway that focus on scaling some proven use cases to drive measurable ROI (e.g., skills coaching, reliable forecasting, or lead routing and scoring).	AI is part of the organization's NDA and is a core business driver that reimagines sales processes and creates new value streams. For example, AI might provide dynamically priced solution bundles, custom-tailoring a package of products, services, and pricing on the fly as the customer's needs are defined.
Data & Analytics	Data is siloed and often of questionable quality. The organization is focused on identifying and cleaning critical data sets for a single pilot project (e.g., prospect database contact enhancement).	Data is being centralized into a more accessible repository. Data governance policies are being implemented. There is a focus on creating reliable, integrated data products for AI use.	Data is a unified, real-time, and trusted enterprise asset. A "semantic layer" makes data easily understandable. There is a focus on leveraging proprietary data and newly created data to create unique insights that drive the business forward in meaningful ways.

Assessment Dimension	Level 1: Foundational (Experiment & Prepare)	Level 2: Advanced (Scale & Routinize)	Level 3: AI-Enabled (Transform & Innovate)
Technology & Infrastructure	The organization uses off-the-shelf AI tools embedded in its existing tech stack (e.g., in its CRM or email system). Its role is basic integration and security vetting; there is no dedicated AI infrastructure.	The organization has invested in scalable cloud platforms (e.g., Azure, AWS, Google Cloud). They're investing in MLOps to manage their AI models. IT builds and maintains a dedicated AI infrastructure.	The organization has an enterprise-wide, integrated AI platform. They are using agentic AI and proprietary models. IT is a co-innovation partner. There is a focus on full-stack integration from prompt engineering to hardware management.
People & Culture	There are pockets of enthusiasm mixed with pockets of skepticism and fear. The organization's focus is on basic AI literacy, explaining "why AI" and addressing concerns around job security.	Targeted upskilling programs are in place (e.g., teaching people how to write great AI chat prompts). The culture encourages "testing and sharing learnings." AI champions are identified and empowered.	Most or all employees are fluent in AI, and the default way of working incorporates AI. Team talent has a mix of AI creators and consumers.

Assessment Dimension	Level 1: Foundational (Experiment & Prepare)	Level 2: Advanced (Scale & Routinize)	Level 3: AI-Enabled (Transform & Innovate)
Governance & Ethics	The organization has no formal policies or informal, ad hoc reviews of specific use cases. Conversations about AI ethics are driven by highly motivated, forward-thinking individuals.	The organization has defined and published ethical principles for its use of AI. A formal AI governance council has been established and is developing processes for bias detection and risk assessment.	Ethical AI practices are deeply embedded in the organization—in fact, they are a default requirement in new systems design. Metrics for fairness, transparency, or ethical compliance issues can block projects from launching or continuing to operate.
Cross-functional Collaboration	*Sales & Marketing:* There are initial talks about using marketing data for a lead scoring pilot. *Sales & IT:* Sales is requesting access to tools and ensuring basic CRM data hygiene.	*Sales & Marketing:* Are jointly defining data requirements for predictive models. *Sales, Marketing, and Finance:* Finance is brought into the mix to build ROI models and secure budgets for formal, scalable AI projects.	*Sales, Marketing, IT, and Finance:* Are operating with a unified "revenue operations" framework. They co-develop proprietary AI solutions and business models, and dynamically allocate company-wide budgets based on AI-driven forecasts.

LEVEL 1: LAYING THE FOUNDATION

The foundational stage of AI readiness is defined by experimentation, preparation, and learning. You're not going to completely revolutionize how sales are done at your organization, but you will learn a bit about how it operates, and will have some small, tangible victories that build momentum and confidence.

In this phase, you're taking a cautious, curious approach—seeing where AI might be able to address some well-understood problems with limited reach. Success in this phase is as much about learning and building enthusiasm across the team as it is about actually changing the nature of your work—but these successes create the cultural and operational groundwork that will support more ambitious projects in the future.

Strategic Vision & Business Alignment

At this stage, the most effective strategy is to avoid "doing an AI project" just because you think you should. Instead, focus on which specific, clearly defined business problems exist that might be made better through AI.

Think particularly about the kinds of high-volume administrative tasks that create a lot of work for sellers, which don't involve much value-added, uniquely human input. By creating real value with these quick wins, you'll have a compelling case to invest further in more complicated AI projects.

Later chapters of this book will provide specific suggestions for projects and tools to consider for different stakeholders at different levels of maturity, but for now, we might think about eliminating the back-and-forth emails for meeting scheduling, summarizing action items from a meeting, or creating first drafts of responses to email queries as candidates for this phase.

Talking widely and publicly about wins from these sorts of projects is a nonthreatening way to introduce AI as simply "a productivity enabler" rather than a more ominous or scary "AI rollout." You'll likely find requests from your team to find more of these kinds of projects, creating a bottom-up groundswell of support for your AI transformation.

Some organizations may find that their first AI projects are started by employees before a strategic AI vision comes down from the executive team. By definition, these organizations are already in the first phases of an AI deployment—and the leadership team will need to act quickly to provide guardrails that ensure the started projects become sanctioned ones. Failing to do so risks an unauthorized shadow deployment of AI tools that employees will use regardless, running the risk that your sensitive company data will wind up in public AI models unchecked.

Data & Analytics

When you're working on the foundational level of AI usage, the main challenge about data is that it is incomplete, inconsistent, and stored in disconnected silos. The result can be a "mile-wide but inch-deep" dataset that lacks the quality or structure needed to do sophisticated analyses.

As you get started with your project, though, don't get bogged down in trying to create a perfectly clean, comprehensive dataset of everything in the sales organization. The guidance that "done is better than perfect" will help you get insights that are "good enough" to advance your business—but you'll want to avoid becoming complacent that "good enough" will be appropriate forever.

In the foundational, experimental stages of AI usage, low-stakes mistakes aren't costly; perhaps a seller wastes 10 minutes chasing a bad lead that was scored incorrectly by an intent algorithm. In later stages, though—when that algorithm is broadly embedded in the day-to-day operations of large teams of sellers—you'll want your tools to operate with more accuracy.

For whatever use case your pilot project tackles, think about what success actually requires, and work to identify and clean the data in just those narrowly defined sources that will support your chosen use case.

For example, a pilot project that is focused on lead scoring should stay focused on just cleaning the historic marketing engagement data (like email opens and website visits) and required CRM contact records (name, email address, and phone), even if other CRM fields like company headquarters address, NAICS codes, or other data are ignored.

By limiting your data cleansing efforts, you'll maintain a manageable approach to data readiness for your pilot project and will speed the time to proving value on this important first foray into using AI.

People & Culture

Projects don't succeed with just a business strategy and technology, though. It's their intersection with humanity—your team members—that will make or break the project's overall success, and the human element is often the most difficult part to manage in the foundational stage of AI rollout.

Team members will have a wide range of feelings about the introduction of new technologies. Some will be excited, eager to be the first to adopt new tools. Many employees will be skeptical of AI tools, and some will be outright fearful of what it means for them, with particular concerns about how their jobs will change or whether they will be entirely eliminated by AI. By clearly identifying and addressing this wide range of emotions, you'll increase your chance of success with both your pilot projects and longer-term AI adoption goals.

This means that having a communication strategy is essential. In conversations with team members, it's helpful to frame AI as a tool that *augments* their jobs—not as one that *automates or replaces* them. Remembering that the most critical part of selling is the human connectedness that AI tools can't replicate, leaders should consistently frame AI as a tool to enhance their human capabilities and judgment—not make them obsolete.

AI tools can be deployed to act as a personal sales coach, serving up data-driven insights during a sales call to help sellers improve their performance, but these tools are not going to run the sales call independently. This is why so many AI tools are branded as "copilots"—they assist with navigation and automate routine checks, while allowing the human pilot to focus on the strategic parts of the journey.

Creating "safe AI playgrounds" where employees can experiment with tools in low-stakes ways while developing new skills can also go a long way toward building employee comfort with AI tools, which will ensure their success later on.

Give them some simple ground rules for operations (no use of real customer names in public AI tools, for example) and create a place for sellers to celebrate their successes. Perhaps a dedicated Slack channel can be set up where sellers share the specific AI prompts or tricks that gave them great results—celebrating the seller, while improving everyone's AI literacy.

Creating a safe space for feedback is also important. Once the leadership team has clearly articulated the objectives of the pilot, the reason the specific technology has been chosen, and the metrics they'll use to evaluate success, they need to create forums for open dialogue about real users' experiences.

These may include large and small group discussions, Slack channels, or other discussion groups where team members can ask questions, share concerns without fear of judgment, and offer suggestions for improvement. AI champions or members of your governance council should commit to acknowledging the feedback, even if they won't act on all suggestions received.

Governance & Ethics

In the foundational stage, AI governance is typically informal and reactive. As they use different tools, individual employees or teams may be driven by their real-world experiences to advocate for various ethical considerations. A seller on the West Coast, for example, might observe that the new AI tool is deprioritizing leads from a certain geographic region and start to investigate why. Ultimately, these sorts of investigations may lead to asking the critical question, "Should we be doing this?" rather than simply "Can we do this?"

In this stage, leadership should encourage and provide legitimacy to these conversations. When we create an environment where employees are empowered to raise ethical concerns, we lay the foundation for the more formal, sophisticated ethics practices we'll need later in our AI journey. And when we gain small wins by resolving small ethical concerns early on—correcting the bias in the lead scoring algorithm, for example—we prove our commitment to using tools appropriately and develop trust among our employees that we will do the right thing.

Cross-functional Collaboration

Even in the foundational stages, you'll find that AI usage isn't something that can be confined to just the world of the sales organization—partnerships with other departments will be required to be successful.

Marketing will be the most critical first partner in your AI journey, and your CMO will be a key person to engage. Many of the valuable first-stage pilots sales teams take on—like lead scoring or personalized outreach—depend on marketing data. If you're not already collaborating with marketing on defining what a qualified lead is, or which personas at which ICPs are worth targeting, these projects will quickly surface those needs.

IT is another key stakeholder in your project, as they're the keeper of the keys to your company's tech ecosystem. Their role is to vet potential vendors for security and compliance issues, manage their integration with existing tools such as your CRM system, and, if needed, negotiate the contracts and procure the selected tools on your organization's behalf. They'll also have invaluable expertise in identifying your data sources, extracting training data, and provisioning ongoing feeds of it for AI use.

Finance may also play a role in the early stages of AI usage. While your initial pilot programs don't likely require large cash outlays, their success will be the core ROI story you use to justify larger-scale investments in the future. Letting your finance peers know what you're working on in this phase can help smooth the path in the future.

LEVEL 2: BUILDING MOMENTUM FOR ADVANCED AI

Once you've gotten some success with small-scale pilots, you'll be eager to move to a more advanced stage of AI usage. In this phase, you're transitioning from a random set of isolated experiments to a more systematic, thoughtful, team-wide use of AI tools. You've already got proof that AI can work in some sales circumstances. This phase is where you start to make it work at scale.

Making the transition to Level 2 sophistication will require more deliberate activity to define your strategic vision, secure your data foundation, invest in highly scalable technology, and ensure every employee is on board for the ride. When you've done so, your AI implementation will not just be a novelty; it will be a real source of competitive advantage for your GTM team.

Strategic Vision & Business Alignment

At the advanced level of AI usage, these tools aren't just side projects—they now have the formal backing of executive sponsorship and resources dedicated to them as a formal strategic initiative.

The vision for your AI projects isn't just solving isolated pain points—it's now moved to creating an integrated system that can help your team across the entire sales cycle—from early lead generation through negotiation and close. You'll know it's a success when you have measurable, positive impacts on key sales metrics such as sales velocity, conversion rates, and forecast accuracy.

At this stage, sales teams often turn to AI for things like lead scoring, sales coaching, and deal forecasting. In doing so, they're not looking to the tools to simply automate or enhance their existing processes—they're looking for actionable insights that can fundamentally redesign and improve them.

When I first encountered forecasting at scale, it was at an organization that had hundreds of sellers. We'd developed a highly complex, manual process by which sellers committed deals to their managers, managers committed rollup numbers to regional VPs, regional VPs reviewed the numbers with the CRO and CFO and then a series of deal inspections and probing calls made their way back down through the organization to ensure we had a number that could confidently be reported to the street.

It was a very manual process—cobbled together from a series of interconnected spreadsheets and a cadence of meetings with different agendas for each day of the week—but it was effective.

Yet using AI to simply replicate or automate this process would miss the point. The real benefit of AI deployment, or any technology deployment, should be to challenge our long-held assumptions and re-architect our work to be more efficient and effective.

Indeed, when I first deployed Clari as my revenue intelligence platform, I found that its ability to analyze historical data to identify which deals look most like the one I'm trying to forecast today helped me create a highly accurate forecast in seconds.

As a result, I no longer needed hours of meetings on my calendar to simply "call what number we will hit," and could redirect that time to coaching sellers on their deals to improve their ultimate results.

Even better, my board learned to trust the accuracy of my Clari-generated forecast, so I no longer had to spend an hour of our time together explaining why I was confident in the number I was forecasting; the news was delivered and accepted in two minutes.

Instead, we spent an hour talking about what we wanted to do about the number we agreed was coming—whether that be spending the money produced by an overperformance against goal or managing costs in response to a projected shortfall.

Having either conversation was good for the business and something that would not have been possible if we hadn't used Clari's AI tool to reimagine our forecasting process.

Data & Analytics

In this second phase of AI sophistication, your data strategy needs to be much more mature than during your foundational pilot stage. No longer is the goal to get "data that is just good enough" for the project—you'll start building a robust, centralized data foundation on clean data with a more all-encompassing scope. This is a major undertaking and will require dedicated resources from multiple, cross-functional teams.

In this phase, you'll want to launch a formal project to consolidate data from across disparate silos—including your CRM system, marketing automation platforms, and customer success tools—creating a unified repository for all customer data. This data set will be what more sophisticated AI tools get trained on, and it's from there that more complex patterns of customer behavior will be identified.

While you're doing this, your organization will also need to establish and enforce a formal data governance policy that sets standards for data quality and identifies who has access to it, in what situations, what it can be used for, and for what length of time.

The result is that your data is not just "exhaust generated as a result of doing business." Instead, it's a curated product in its own right, specifically developed and managed to be consumed by your strategic AI toolset.

Technology & Infrastructure

As the scale of your AI projects increases, so will your need for data storage and analysis power. At Level 2, your IT team will move beyond simply vetting tools to begin architecting a scalable cloud foundation—leveraging platforms like Microsoft Azure, Amazon Web Services (AWS), or Google Cloud. These platforms provide the high-performance processing and enterprise-grade security necessary to deploy and train complex AI models across a global sales team.

This stage also forces a critical strategic choice: will you adopt an all-in-one suite of tools, or create an integrated "best-of-breed" tech stack from multiple vendors?

The suite approach emphasizes a single-vendor offering that incorporates AI capabilities across an entire platform (often with varying degrees of success), based on the promise of seamless integration and a single "throat to choke."

The best-of-breed approach integrates specialized tools—such as a dedicated forecasting platform and a niche conversational intelligence tool—in the hopes that a higher investment in integration and technical management will result in a significant performance advantage.

Finally, Level 2 maturity marks the introduction of machine learning operations processes (MLOps). These are the rigorous procedures used to automate the deployment, monitoring, and continuous retraining of your AI models to keep them accurate and relevant over time.

People & Culture

While your early experiments with AI may have flown under the radar, the more widespread use of these tools in the second phase of sophistication will need a lot more cultural attention. Your focus will shift from overcoming early fears about the technology to creating new skill sets and competencies across the entire organization.

Your upskilling efforts will need to move beyond basic AI literacy to more targeted, role-specific training. Each role in the sales organization needs to know when to use AI tools and the specific steps to take as they do. Naming and empowering "AI champions" in each role can be helpful—they'll provide on-the-ground resources to share success stories, serve as peer mentors, and offer real-time training and assistance to teammates.

While I don't love the reputation of salespeople as "coin operated," there is some truth to the fact that workers (in any role) focus on the behaviors that their compensation plans are aligned with. With this in mind, you'll want to work with your HR team to be sure the new job requirements from AI use are incorporated into your evaluation and payment plans.

Do you need CSRs to maintain a specific data field in a specific way for the AI model to work? Be sure it's part of their performance review. The same is true for sellers, managers, and leaders who have a part to play in the overall AI program's success.

Middle managers, in particular, will be a focus of this work. Historically, these professionals have served as information gatekeepers—organizational bottlenecks where data is collected from frontline sellers, scrubbed in spreadsheets, and repackaged for executive consumption. When AI tools begin performing these tasks with greater speed and accuracy, it may be painful—or threatening—to managers who have equated "controlling the data" with "having job security."

To manage this transition successfully, your leaders need to not just encourage the management class—their role will fundamentally evolve. You'll want to shift their performance reviews' success metrics away from administrative oversight and toward high-leverage activities only a human can do—providing nuanced coaching to sellers, developing strategies for complex deals, and developing junior talent.

There is a significant risk here that is easy to overlook. Many of your best middle managers may have been promoted because they were masters at manipulating all of your manual spreadsheets and data, and they may not naturally possess the high-level coaching skills you are now demanding of them.

To keep them relevant, you must invest in coaching for this cohort of management coaches. If you simply change their KPIs without providing them with the development they need to become elite mentors, they will feel exposed and vulnerable.

As a result, you risk having a middle-management team that either quietly sabotages the AI rollout in hopes of preserving their jobs or a team that fills their newly reclaimed time with all types of administrative "busywork" to prove that they are still important.

Governance & Ethics

As your AI deployment expands, so do the associated risks. In the foundational phase, governance may have been reactive. In the advanced phase, it must become a proactive part of your project—you must establish a formal, cross-functional governance council or "AI center of excellence" to set clear guidelines for AI usage that can tie it to corporate objectives.

The council should not be a purely technical or legal body—it requires a group of stakeholders who understand both the mechanics of the risks and the mission of the sales team. It should include representatives from:

- Sales & marketing, who ensure the guardrails don't stifle revenue growth or customer experience
- Legal & compliance, who help navigate the ever-evolving landscape of data privacy laws and AI-specific regulations

- HR, who will manage the "people and culture" shifts, and make sure that AI isn't introducing hidden biases into hiring or performance evaluations
- IT & security, who will maintain data integrity and prevent unofficial, "shadow AI" deployments from creating security vulnerabilities

The council's mandate is to define and publish the company's official AI ethics principles. These typically focus on promoting three goals:

1. **Fairness: Guarding Against Revenue-Killing Biases**

   Bias in AI isn't just a social issue; it's a business failure. If your lead-scoring algorithm inadvertently deprioritizes a certain geography or demographic because of flawed historical data, you aren't just being "unfair"—you are actively leaving money on the table. The council must regularly audit models to ensure they aren't creating "digital redlining" that prevents your team from seeing valid opportunities.

2. **Transparency: Addressing the "Black Box" Problem**

   Sales professionals are naturally skeptical. If an AI tool tells a seller to "target this prospect" or "offer this additional discount" without explaining why, the seller will likely ignore the advice. Transparency (or "explainability") ensures that users understand the logic behind a recommendation. For governance to work, the AI's "reasoning" must be interpretable enough that any user can defend an AI-driven decision to their manager or customer.

3. **Accountability: Defining Where the Buck Stops**

   Who is responsible when an AI-generated outreach email hallucinates a feature that doesn't exist or promises an unauthorized discount? Accountability establishes clear ownership, and at Level 2, the policy should be clear: **AI is a tool, but the human is the fiduciary.** Leadership must define the "human-in-the-loop" requirements that ensure a person has reviewed and taken responsibility for high-stakes AI outputs before they reach a customer.

The most common mistake at Level 2 is treating governance as the "final hurdle" before launch, which can lead to costly delays when a project is found to be noncompliant after months of development.

Instead, the council should be incorporated at the start of a project to bake ethics reviews and bias assessments into each step of development. By building in "ethics by design," you ensure your AI tools are robust, trustworthy, and reliable from day one—avoiding legal troubles and building trust with all stakeholders along the way.

Cross-functional Collaboration

As AI solutions move into more of your company's standard operating procedures, it will become even more important to have strong collaboration with leaders from other teams, and the boundaries between sales, marketing, and IT will begin to blur as they coalesce around a shared, AI-driven mission for supporting sales.

In the foundational stage, **IT** acted as a gatekeeper for security and procurement. At this stage, they will move from being an approver or facilitator of off-the-shelf tools to a role as a strategic builder and architect. They'll ultimately be responsible for designing, implementing, and managing the scalable cloud infrastructure and MLOps processes that are at the heart of your AI strategy.

Finance will also become a crucial partner, as your AI investment grows from small pilot projects to significant investments in software and infrastructure. As with any investment, expect your CFO to pay careful attention to the return on this investment. That means your sales leader should expect to be working closely with them to identify tangible business outcomes from AI deployments.

The partnership with **marketing** will also grow deeper as you get more sophisticated AI strategies in your GTM program. The marketing team is the primary source of a lot of data—including top-of-funnel and customer engagement data—and they'll collaborate closely with sales on customer segmentation strategies, message personalization, lead scoring, and routing.

Customer success—if not already a part of your GTM organization—will also become a key collaborator in this phase of AI sophistication. By connecting CS and sales leadership around customer-facing AI projects, you ensure they're not just deployments for "new logo wins" but ones that create maximal lifetime value through the entire customer lifecycle.

As your AI project teams collaborate across these organizational boundaries, it will be important to develop a common language and translate key terms between departments. Finance talks about "EBITDA and ROI," IT talks about "latency and models," and sales talks about "booked and recognized revenue." Time spent helping one another understand what these terms actually mean will guide what the AI system is meant to solve for.

LEVEL 3: THE FULLY ENABLED SALES TEAM

The most sophisticated sales teams will see AI as more than a simple tool—it will be an always-on, difference-defining way of doing business. In these organizations, decision-making across every part of the sales function is data-driven and AI-informed, enabling AI insights to drive innovative new business models and value streams based on proprietary intelligence.

Strategic Vision & Business Alignment

For fully AI-enabled organizations, the strategic vision is no longer about improving an existing sales engine; it's about building an entirely new one—and AI is the disruptive force that makes it happen. Companies that get this right may find they can package their AI-enabled sales processes as products to offer other companies, or start pricing their products based on guaranteed outcomes, rather than subscription access.

Fully enabled strategies may involve agentic forms of AI—autonomous AI agents that can follow complex workflows with little human oversight. Perhaps they advance prospects through multiple steps of the lead generation process, or they engage in early, personalized email conversations so that sellers can dedicate their time to building higher-value strategic relationships and managing complex deals.

Creating a proprietary repository of insights specific to your company's offerings and idiosyncrasies may also be part of the fully AI-enabled business. Drawing from your proprietary data on customer usage patterns, meeting transcriptions, and email interactions, you might use AI to create a dynamic, hyper-personalized customer journey that anticipates customer needs and proactively delivers the right message to the right person at the right time—truly differentiating you from your competitors with cost-effective, individualized service.

Data & Analytics

At Level 3, the organization treats data as a value-creating, offering-differentiating enterprise asset. It is no longer just a collection of records—it is the intellectual property that fuels your competitive advantage.

The key to Level 3 deployment is the "semantic layer." This is a sophisticated translation layer that sits on top of your data stores and maps technical data points to easy-to-understand business concepts (like "ideal customer profile," "product/market fit," "churn risk," or "upsell potential").

Semantic layers serve two critical purposes. First, they provide context for AI tools that prevent them from making nonsensical correlations. Second, they empower any human user—from an entry-level BDR to the chairman of the board—to get meaningful responses to natural language questions (like "Show me all accounts in southern states that have a CFO that previously bought from us at another company") without needing to understand the underlying database architecture.

Level 3 maturity also often includes the use of "synthetic data." Here, AI generates new data that mimics the statistical properties of your actual customer base, allowing leadership teams to run hypothetical "what if" scenarios without ever compromising real customer data. Using a "digital twin" of your production sales systems, your leaders might evaluate the effects of new pricing models, territory assignments, or marketing tactics through simulations of dozens of different possibilities before choosing their real-world course of action.

Technology & Infrastructure

At Level 3, the organization moves beyond "adding AI features" to maintaining a tech stack that is "AI native." In these environments, AI capabilities are not just embedded; they are the foundational architecture upon which all other tools are built. There is no longer a distinction between "the AI environment" and "the rest of the tech environment." The technology itself is designed to perceive, reason, and act.

To get there, Level 3 organizations achieve "agentic mesh." Instead of isolated tools that require a human to copy and paste data between them, the stack consists of autonomous agents that orchestrate work across the enterprise.

For example, when a "prospecting agent" identifies a high-intent signal from a website visitor, it doesn't just send an alert—it autonomously triggers a "research agent" to build a profile, prompts a "content agent" to draft a hyper-personalized pitch, and updates the CRM with a calling task for the BDR—all before the human seller is aware of the new prospect.

At Level 3, the technology also disappears into the workflow. Sellers rarely need to manually log into a CRM to update a field or pull a report because their AI infrastructure has captured relevant data through ambient sensing—recording calls, analyzing emails, and tracking deal progress—and updated the "system of record" automatically. In Level 3 organizations, technology serves the seller rather than the seller serving technology.

Finally, while Level 1 and 2 organizations use "off-the-shelf" models purchased from outside vendors, Level 3 organizations are likely fine-tuning their own proprietary models. By training AI on your specific successful sales methodologies, unique product nuances, and historical customer interactions, IT creates a "company-specific brain" that provides strategic guidance no generic, public AI could ever match.

People & Culture

In fully AI-enabled organizations, the default mode of operating is always a partnership between people and AI tools. Employees are recruited and trained for this ability, so the fears and skepticism of the earlier stages are replaced by a serious embrace of AI-enabled work.

This means that recruiting and training programs are no longer just looking for closers for the sales team—they're looking for "orchestrators of AI processes." These professionals are effective sellers, in part, because they can effectively direct autonomous agents and interpret complex data analysis while doubling down on their uniquely human skill set to continue customer engagement where technology's capabilities naturally end.

New roles may also be developed in "AI creation" roles (like data scientists, AI ethicists, and MLOps professionals), whose sole role is to fine-tune the proprietary models that drive your unique sales methodology. These professionals ensure that AI tools aren't just working, but are perfectly aligned with the nuanced brand voice and ethical standards of your company.

As AI increasingly takes on the administrative tasks as the "lowest cost resource capable of doing" any number of jobs, the sales professional becomes increasingly defined by abilities that are uniquely human. Skills such as empathy, multi-stakeholder political navigation, and strategic hypothesis generation become even more valuable assets and are awarded accordingly.

Governance & Ethics

In a fully AI-enabled organization, ethical considerations are part of every process in the department. As such, governance may shift from a central council to one that embeds ethics and AI specialists in each team to provide real-time guidance.

In such organizations, metrics related to fairness, bias, and transparency are tracked as rigorously as profit and revenue, and projects to maximize them carry just as much weight.

Cross-functional Collaboration

In a fully AI-enabled organization, a number of silos have been completely eliminated.

Sales and marketing operate as a single cohesive go-to-market organization that seamlessly moves customers through the customer journey in an AI-informed way. Real-time insights from sales conversations are fed back to adjust marketing campaigns, while real-time marketing analytics can dynamically reprioritize sellers' time to the most productive prospects.

IT is a thought partner to the business—co-developing systems and processes that use AI to create competitive advantage in the marketplace.

Finance is also a strong collaborator with sales—using real-time forecasts to confidently adjust spending levels on new initiatives that will drive the business forward.

These are hard—some may say unrealistic—goals to achieve. Becoming a fully AI-enabled organization will take a long time, and you may never fully get there. But there are significant benefits even in the earliest steps of this transformation—and it's worth the effort to start the journey now.

In the next chapters, we'll look team by team at some quick, foundational wins to be had with AI today, along with a developmental roadmap through more sophisticated use cases to grow into.

AI FOR THE QUOTA-CARRYING SELLER

For as long as I can remember, quota-carrying sellers have found their days consumed with administrivia. List building and research tasks are important to the seller's success, but they're manual, time-consuming processes that leave little time to actually engage with customers and prospects.

With AI now available as the ultimate low-cost resource to take on these data-intensive functions, frontline sellers suddenly have a historic opportunity to delegate the digital heavy lifting to an algorithm, while reclaiming their time to do only what a human can—communicate with nuance, build deep trust, and navigate the complex interpersonal politics needed to close large deals.

This chapter moves beyond AI theory into the trenches—following a typical "day in the life" of a seller with practical, tactical opportunities to use AI every step of the way.

MORNING PREP: AI FOR PLANNING AND PRIORITIZATION

For many sellers, the day begins with a seemingly infinite scroll of uncertainty. They open their laptop, log into their CRM system, find a target list of hundreds of accounts and not nearly enough strong opportunities, and wonder, "Where should I begin today?"

Their answer usually comes from gut instinct, whichever email is at the top of the inbox, and a focus on whatever deals feel "hottest" at the moment. The result is that the loudest, most urgent prospects get attention—but perhaps not the most important ones.

AI tools can provide structure and clarity to this process—sifting through email and CRM data, scoring each prospect and opportunity, and surfacing the most critical signals to a pre-vetted, prioritized action list for the seller to get to work on at the start of the day.

Predictive Lead & Opportunity Scoring

At its core, prioritization is about placing bets on where to spend the limited resource of your time, and predictive scoring is how AI can help you know where to place them.

Many companies use a rules-based approach to lead scoring reminiscent of the first-generation, good old-fashioned, symbolic AI ("award 10 points if the company is in the Fortune 500, add another 10 points if they've filled out a form on our website in the last three days," and so on).

Today's AI algorithms, however, can look at each of your opportunities' demographic characteristics and real-time engagement data, compare them against similar data from every opportunity your company has ever won or lost, and create a dynamic score for each lead to assess your likelihood of winning it—and, therefore, where to focus your time to have the biggest impact.

Level 1: Foundational

The easiest way to get started is to explore the native scoring features in your existing CRM system.

In a platform like **HubSpot Sales Hub**, an administrator can set up scoring criteria based on demographic properties (such as company industry codes or employee counts) and behavioral data (such as website visits, email opens, or form submissions). Enterprise subscribers get access to an AI-assisted scoring feature that can analyze the history of converted contacts to automatically recommend which criteria are most predictive—taking the guesswork out of this setup.

For **Salesforce** users, an **Einstein** Lead Score is a similar machine-learning prediction. If your organization doesn't have enough historical data to build a custom model, you can get an immediate start from a global model that is based on the anonymized data from thousands of other Salesforce customers.

An individual seller may not be able to turn on this functionality themselves, but your CRM admins should be able to enable this functionality for sellers with relative ease.

Level 2: Advanced

While native CRM scoring functionality is a great place to start, dedicated revenue intelligence platforms can take this a step further by bringing in data from a wider variety of data sources.

Platforms like **Clari** and **Gong** can generate sophisticated deal health scores by integrating your CRM data with unstructured conversational data extracted from call recordings and email conversations. Clari's "AI Advanced Opportunity Scores" give you a live pulse of deal health based on the sentiment and topics of recent conversations, while Gong's "Deal Warnings" might flag a deal as at-risk if pricing was discussed but no next steps have been set since last week's conversation. **Outreach** provides similar signals through its "Smart Deal Assist" functionality, which recommends actions to keep deals on track.

Revenue intelligence platforms like these are typically deployed alongside (and integrated with) your CRM, email, and calendaring tools—and need widespread adoption by the entire sales team to provide meaningful value, but are straightforward projects for organizations to implement.

Level 3: AI-Enabled

When a seller's daily work plan is proactively built by an AI tool (instead of just providing insight to inform human decision-makers), their organization has moved to the highest level of AI sophistication. This requires a high level of trust in the AI's recommendations, an organizational willingness to change how sellers work, and a deep level of integration across the tech stack.

An example of this change is **Salesloft's** "Rhythm" workflow, which claims to use AI to pull signals from across the tech stack to create a focused, ranked list of actions for sellers to take.

The result isn't just a dashboard of deals and scores—it's a directive task list for the seller to follow, like "Call these two people, send an email to these five, and start prepping for this demo."

Outreach indicates that they're aiming to create a similar single, intelligent work queue to guide sellers through their day.

As your organization considers AI tools for lead scoring, your governance council must think carefully about the quality of the data sources informing these suggestions—and collaborate across the sales, marketing, and RevOps teams to get the inputs right.

The old axiom "garbage in, garbage out" is especially important for AI—getting the signal data wrong leads to poor conclusions that send sellers down a dead-end path. To succeed, you need to make sure that your data is as reliable as the human judgment it is meant to augment.

Surfacing Buyer Intent

While predictive scoring helps prioritize time amongst companies you already know about, intent data tells you which companies you don't yet know that are actively looking for a solution like yours right now. AI-powered "buyer intent" platforms monitor billions of online signals across the web to surface these for you by seeing who is doing online searches for specific topics, reading product review articles, or visiting relevant websites.

When we use tools like these, our cold outreach becomes a lot warmer—as we're calling relevant people right at the moment they're researching products or competitors online.

Level 2: Advanced

While the commitment to intent provider data is one that needs to be made team-wide, it's still fairly straightforward to subscribe to a provider such as **6sense, ZoomInfo,** or **Cognism/Bombora** and integrate it into your CRM or sales engagement platform.

Once set up, sellers or marketers can receive alerts that identify which target accounts' web-wide behaviors suggest they might be "in market."

For example, anonymous research behavior might suggest that people at a target organization's domain are starting to run searches on your top competitor. When you launch a proactive outreach campaign as a result, you're no longer making guesses about who to call; you're engaging with accounts right at the time they're entering the buying journey.

Level 3: AI-Enabled

When organizations take this one step further by deploying agents that automatically respond based on these signals, they've moved into the AI-enabled level of usage. For example, they may configure a **6sense** rule that says "When any Tier 1 target account shows a spike in intent for my product's pain points, automatically identify the VP of finance in the organization and enroll them in an Outreach sequence that explains my related value prop."

In this example, a human has identified the strategy and approved the messaging, but an AI agent is doing continuous, real-time monitoring and execution. Implementing this confidently requires an organization-wide commitment to the strategy; tight, reliable integration between your intent and engagement platforms; and sophisticated workflow automation capabilities.

To use buyer intent effectively, your council will want to guide how deeply and quickly these signals make their way into human-led connections. Calling a prospect and saying, "I see that you just ran a search for my product," is downright creepy and is likely to have the opposite of the intended effect on your sales process.

Moreover, as laws such as the EU AI Act and CCPA evolve, the ethics of de-anonymizing web signals will likely be subject to heightened scrutiny. To stay on the right side of the law and your customer's expectations, create a process where data prompts sellers to have more helpful human conversations—but don't create the impression of digital stalking.

THE PROSPECTING POWER HOUR: AI FOR FINDING AND QUALIFYING LEADS

Once a seller has prioritized their accounts for the day, they need to identify the right people inside those accounts and reach out to them with targeted messaging informed by thorough research.

For most sellers, there aren't enough hours in the day to develop truly personalized messaging—so they fall back on generic "Saw we went to the same school," or "I also work in the financial industry" kinds of "personalization" with limited effectiveness.

By using AI as a copilot, though, sellers can generate hyper-targeted messages to contacts with verified contact data—using deep research to personalize outreach with relevant, meaningful messages.

Building and Enriching Lists

It starts with generating a well-targeted prospect list with accurate contact information—and AI has made building and enriching these lists fast and effective. While many tools have commoditized the ability to identify basic contact information, the most innovative approaches come from using actionable insights about those contacts to begin a truly meaningful conversation with them.

Level 1: Foundational

One of the easiest ways for sellers to incorporate AI into this process is to install a browser extension that can surface email addresses and phone numbers for individual contacts, right as they're looking at a prospect's LinkedIn profile.

Products like **Wiza, RocketReach, Apollo.io,** and **Seamless.AI** offer individual users "freemium" access to get started, while tools like **ZoomInfo** and **Cognism** are typically purchased at an organizational level. Offering one-click integration to import their data into CRM or engagement tools can save sellers hours of manual data processing time each week.

Level 2: Advanced

More advanced tools use AI to automate the research and enrichment on an entire list of contacts, rather than one at a time. **Clay** offers sellers a waterfall workflow builder, which might begin with 100 target companies, and then a series of cascading rules like "Find the VP of marketing. If none is found, find the most senior marketing director. Then visit their LinkedIn profile, read their three most recent posts, and use a large language model to create the text of a personalized icebreaker email message."

ZoomInfo's Copilot offers a similar ability to generate personalized messages, as does **Cognism**'s Cortex AI, which generates summaries of the target company's business model, recent news, and strategic priorities to guide the messaging.

In assessing your readiness for this use case through a data and analytics lens, you'll want to tread carefully around issues that may affect your

Case Study: Scaling Growth Experiments with AI-Driven Personalization

The Challenge

A multi-product SaaS platform (valued at $10B+) needed to scale its outbound motion across several distinct product lines (HR, IT, and finance). Their growth team was stuck in a "high-volume, low-relevance" cycle because manual research on thousands of prospects was impossible, but generic automation was being ignored by their sophisticated buyer personas.

The Solution: AI-Driven Prospect Identification

The company replaced traditional static lists with a dynamic workflow:

- **Finding contacts:** They built a cascading logic to identify the highest-ranking decision-maker. If a "VP of IT" was unavailable, the system automatically hunted for a "Director of IT," and then a "Head of Infrastructure."

- **Deep AI enrichment:** Once the contact was found, an AI agent was deployed to visit the company's website and the individual's LinkedIn profile.

- **Signal scraping:** The AI tool was trained to look for specific "triggers," such as a recent office expansion, a new funding round, or specific technologies mentioned in job postings.

- **LLM personalization:** Each of these data points (the title, the specific trigger, and the company's focus) was fed into a large language model. The LLM then drafted a one-to-one icebreaker message that connected the prospect's current initiatives to a specific product module.

The ROI

- **2x increase in outbound performance:** The company saw a 100% improvement in cold email conversion rates.

> - **Operational efficiency:** They fully automated a research process that previously required an army of sales development representatives (SDRs) or expensive, time-consuming manual audits.
> - **Agility:** The growth team could now launch and test a new "experiment" (e.g., a new niche industry campaign) in hours rather than weeks.

organization's email domain reputation. Depending on the approach you use for AI-based data enrichment, you may find a certain lack of data cleanliness is "good enough" for a small-scale pilot—but when your entire sales team is using the same process to send hundreds or thousands of messages, it is no longer acceptable.

If a person (or their AI agent) aggressively emails prospects based on outdated or incorrect CRM data (sending to an address that no longer exists—or never did), their messages generate hard bounces.

Similarly, if their messaging misses the mark enough that prospects flag them as "spam" (perhaps they're sending hallucinated, irrelevant messages at scale), the organization's sender reputation degrades—making it more likely that any email from the organization (AI-generated or not) gets stuck in spam filters.

Level 3: AI-Enabled

At the highest level of sophistication, an organization might deploy an AI agent that autonomously builds and maintains the entire prospect database on the sellers' behalf, based on a clearly defined ICP and real-time trigger events.

Such agents—built on a platform like **Clay** or through a combination of tools and APIs—would continuously monitor a wide variety of data sources for triggers relevant to your sales process (like M&A activity, executive hires, or purchase of a key partner's product).

When one of these triggering events is identified at a company that matches your ICP, the agent automatically identifies all personas likely to be on the evaluation committee, enriches their contact data, adds them to CRM as high-priority targets, and launches an engagement campaign under the appropriate seller's name.

While these processes can be helpful when deployed correctly, your governance council will also want to ensure that real-life, thinking humans are in the loop to monitor the process. AI can easily detect that a business or executive is "in the news," but may lack the nuanced "social awareness" to discriminate between a celebratory expansion and a personal legal scandal. Requiring a socially aware human to evaluate and launch outreach can help prevent tone-deaf misfires that would transform a "personalized message" into an embarrassing brand liability.

CRAFTING THE PERFECT OUTREACH: AI FOR PERSONALIZED ENGAGEMENT AT SCALE

A few years ago, I realized that someone must have told sellers that, to cut through the clutter in an executive's inbox, they needed to create a personalized message in their first sentence. I started collecting examples of poorly done personalization in a folder that I called my "hall of shame" to share with my own sales teams. They often were poorly mail-merged or found tenuous connections in their attempts to build rapport:

- "Hi MILLER: I'm writing today because …"
- "Jd, I'm such a fan of what you're doing over there at Motus …"
- "I see you're a technology executive in the Midwest. I am too!"
- "Did you see what the Celtics did last night?" (I'm a Chicago native …)
- "I see you graduated from the University of Illinois. Go Illini!"
- "I'm looking to connect with like-minded individuals …"

I understand how these messages came to be—sellers wanted to do *something* to stand out, but didn't have the time to really read the LinkedIn profiles or executive bios of the hundred or so people they had on their contact list for the day—and so grabbed a few easy-to-extract data fields and hoped for the best.

With generative AI, though, these sellers have access to a personal research and writing assistant that moves beyond these superficial hooks—and potentially does so with better grammar and spelling too.

When it's done well, the professional is truly engaging in "social selling"—using social media clues to connect with prospects in a truly personal way.

When incorporating these tools, though, sellers should be aware that hyper-personalization comes with risks. While bonding over a truly shared experience or interest can help to build trust between buyer and seller, prospects who realize that a "personal" note was generated by an algorithm that scraped the web for semi-private information can easily feel betrayed—and wind up distrusting the seller instead.

With this in mind, you might consider a governance model for AI personalization tools that says personalization based on professional data points like 10-K filings, press releases, or patent filings is appropriate for use in outreach, but personal data scraped from nonprofessional social media, personal family photos, or private location data is off-limits.

The goal of social selling is not to "trick" a prospect into thinking that you're their best friend. It's to prove that you've done enough homework to be a valuable professional partner in a way that only a human can be.

THE AI EMAIL ASSISTANT

Sellers may find that this is best done by using AI to provide them with insights for outreach messages that they write themselves—and one class of tools provides writing assistance from within your inbox or sales engagement platform to help sellers write better, faster.

These tools can generate first drafts of email messages, rewrite existing messages with a more professional tone, check for words that might trigger spam filters, or suggest personalized icebreakers based on the recipient's online activity.

Level 1: Foundational

One of the easiest places to start is from a native plugin in your inbox. Gmail users might use the **Gemini** plugin to polish their email message, or a seller might prompt **ChatGPT** to "Draft a three-sentence response" to a message that just landed in their Outlook inbox, raising the quality of their writing in the process.

Writing coaches like **Lavender,** which provide readability scores or offer suggestions for personalizing messages based on publicly available data about the recipient, also fall in this Level 1 category, as do the writing support features in **HubSpot** AI Assistant and **Regie.ai**.

Often deployed as simple browser extensions with free or affordable monthly plans, these tools can be installed and used by individual sellers with little to no training.

Level 2: Advanced

At the next level of sophistication, advanced AI use cases leverage generative AI to create multistep, multichannel outreach campaigns from a simple prompt.

Sales engagement platforms like **Outreach, Salesloft,** or **Regie.ai** can offer professionals the ability to create detailed prompts like "Create a 15-step, multichannel sequence that targets the CFO of a retail company. The sequence should focus on the problems of inventory shrinkage and abandoned online carts, and should include five emails, five phone call tasks, two LinkedIn connection requests, and invitations to our next three industry-specific webinars."

Once prompted, the AI tools can generate the entire campaign, with draft copy at each step for the seller to review, edit, and launch. In doing so, the professional will save hours of creative effort and can be confident that they're adhering to brand standards and proven best practices.

Recognizing that spam filters are increasingly good at detecting mass mail campaigns, tools like **Reply.io** offer message designers the opportunity to insert "AI variables" into their templates that get replaced by unique, personalized messaging for every prospect enrolled in a campaign.

Deploying an AI-based sales engagement platform is typically done at the organizational level through a company-wide subscription, and users will be most effective if they've received training on how to best prompt the AI tools to achieve their goals.

Level 3: AI-Enabled

At the most advanced level, AI agents don't just write content for an outreach campaign; they independently manage the initial stages of the conversations that result from it.

As prospects reply to messages in the sequence, AI agents might recognize common objections ("I don't have budget for this"), or simple requests ("Can you send me a case study?") and then draft a response for a human seller to approve, or—in some cases—respond automatically based on a predefined set of rules.

For conversations where the prospect expresses clear positive intent ("I'd like to learn more, can we schedule a call?"), the agent might offer the seller's availability via Calendly or seamlessly hand off the conversation to the seller to continue independently.

Solutions like **Reply.io**'s Jason AI or **Qualified**'s PiperX are marketed as "AI SDRs" that can handle these tasks, as are platforms like **Lindy.ai** and **6sense**'s AI Email Agents.

This is another place where you'll want to think carefully about how to maintain trust with your prospects—and weigh whether these agents need to disclose that they are not real people. In some jurisdictions, disclosing that a user is interacting with a bot is a legal requirement. Regardless of local law, however, prospects may feel tricked or betrayed if they engage in an extended interaction with an AI persona, only to find out later it wasn't "real."

The governance council must decide: Do your agents "pretend to be human" to increase open rates, or do they disclose their identity to preserve long-term trust? The decision will determine whether your bot has a photo and a name, like "Sarah, from Catalyst Ink," or is "John, JD's digital assistant."

They'll want to be sure they're staying current with legal developments, too. As voice cloning and AI-generated video capabilities evolve, sellers may soon be sending personalized video messages and voicemails at scale. However, this new use case carries significant legal implications regarding consent and "right of publicity."

The Tennessee ELVIS Act is one example of emerging legislation that protects an individual's voice and likeness from unauthorized AI simulation—and your legal representative on the council will want to establish protocols for avatar-based outreach as these "personality rights" continue to evolve.

Ultimately, handing over outreach to agentic tools requires a high level of trust in your internal guardrails. Because these agents act as the face of your organization at the front line of sales, their deployment requires enterprise-wide approval and rigorous governance to ensure every interaction remains legal, on-brand, and appropriate.

HAVING GREAT CONVERSATIONS

Building connection and interpersonal trust through communication is a fundamentally human task unlikely to be completely replaced by AI.

Case Study: Scaling Pipeline with Autonomous AI Email Agents

The Challenge

A leading enterprise SaaS provider in the pricing and commercial excellence space had a new SDR team that lacked the bandwidth to engage every lead with the necessary depth and persistence as they came up to speed on a complex product set. Manual follow-up was inconsistent, and valuable leads were frequently lost during the transition from marketing interest to sales engagement.

The company needed a way to maintain a high-quality, two-way dialogue with thousands of prospects simultaneously without dramatically increasing its headcount.

The Solution: The Autonomous Conversation Engine

The company implemented an AI-driven conversational email agent designed to act as a digital extension of its sales team.

- **Knowledge-based training:** The agent was trained on the company's product suite, specific industry value propositions, and successful past sales rebuttals.

- **Autonomous two-way dialogue:** Unlike standard outbound sequences that stop when the prospect asks a question, this agent independently engaged in back-and-forth. It recognized a prospect's intent, answered specific product questions, and addressed common objections (such as "not the right time" or "we already have a solution") using the knowledge base it was trained on.

- **Persistence without fatigue:** The agent handled the "heavy lifting" of follow-up—often sending six to eight personalized touches over several weeks—tasks that a human sales development representative often abandons due to time constraints.

> - **The "hot handoff":** The agent sought signs of buying intent, such as "Tell me more" or "What is your pricing?" The moment a prospect expressed a desire to talk, the agent seamlessly alerted an SDR to step in and schedule the meeting.
>
> ### The ROI
>
> - **3x SDR capacity:** The AI agent's output and engagement levels were calculated to be the equivalent of adding three full-time, high-performing SDRs to the team.
> - **10% increase in conversion rate:** Using the AI agent resulted in 10% more suspects converting into sales-qualified opportunities.
> - **Engagement breakthroughs:** The team successfully booked nine high-level meetings in the first 30 days, from a pool of leads previously considered "unreachable" through manual efforts.

Yet, even as we put sellers center stage for this critical piece of the sales process, AI can ensure they're well-prepared, receive real-time coaching and information during their calls, and have follow-up tasks such as summarizing to-dos or updating CRM taken care of automatically.

PRE-MEETING PREP

In my early days of selling, it was hard to know much about the people or companies we were going to meet. An essential part of our sales process, then, was to spend a great deal of our first meeting in discovery—asking for an overview of the business, who the players were, and what key challenges or critical pain points they were experiencing.

Today's buyers have no time for this. You can learn almost anything you want to know about your prospects online in a matter of minutes—from the latest financial reports and employee hires at the company to the individual's professional milestones and public contributions. As a result, sellers simply can't show up to meetings without good research and a strong point of view—and AI can help.

Level 1: Foundational

The earliest versions of **ChatGPT** used training models that resulted in a "knowledge cutoff date"—after which the system was unaware of any new news and information. Yet later versions of the tool (and generative AI tools like it) gained the ability to perform web searches to augment their knowledge in real time, allowing them to answer questions that require current information, such as stock prices, breaking news, or recent events.

As a result, it's now trivially easy for sellers to use these tools for meeting prep help, with a simple prompt like "I'm having a meeting with JD Miller in Chicago. Please prepare me for my sales call." In less than a minute, a briefing can be provided that provides news headlines, key biographical details, and other helpful background information.

Human judgment plays an important role here. I happen to know that I'm one of at least *nine* JD Millers who live in Chicago, and your AI research tool may have trouble figuring out which one you're interested in.

Including a LinkedIn profile link or URL of the prospect's website may help provide more clarity—and if you provide a link to your own, the model will make some suggestions of particular points of connection between you, suggesting potential pain points the prospect may have, along with the relevant product or service offerings from your company to discuss.

Armed with these suggestions, the seller's value isn't in simply regurgitating them to the prospect. It's in curating them—with the perspective taking and real understanding only a human can possess—to arrive at a genuine human connection.

Level 2: Advanced

Organizations can take this one step further by providing access to their internal data systems. For example, **Outreach**'s Smart Account Assist can provide sellers a summary of recent account engagement—pulling from recent emails and transcripts of recent calls and meetings—alongside answers to key questions like "What are my next steps?" or "What potential risks exist in this deal?"

Tools like **Cirrus Insight**'s Meeting AI connect to the seller's calendar to automatically look ahead to booked meetings, proactively compiling a summary for the seller in advance of the call.

When these summaries also include fresh information drawn from web searches, sellers can show up for calls remembering "Here's what we talked about last week—and here's a news article from this morning that makes our previous conversation even more urgent."

As you look to AI tools to integrate public and private knowledge in this way, your governance council must ensure you are using sanctioned, enterprise-grade tools. These systems are designed to isolate sensitive company and prospect data, ensuring that information you're legally obligated to protect never leaks into public training models.

Integrating your data correctly can be a powerful advantage to your sellers—but your chief information security officer and corporate counsel will have legitimate legal concerns that must also be satisfied.

IN-MEETING INTELLIGENCE

Level 1: Foundational

Increases in computing power have enabled AI tools to process more data faster, making them relevant in real-time conversations.

At the foundational level, this makes real-time transcription and note-taking possible, and sellers should take advantage of the built-in services of **Microsoft Teams, Zoom, Google Meet,** or their favorite meeting tools.

Level 2: Advanced

When companies augment those tools with access to their sales playbook, product descriptions, and sales methodologies, these transcripts can also provide real-time coaching to sellers in the call.

When conversational intelligence tools like **Gong, Outreach**'s Kaia, **Clari** Copilot, **Avoma,** or **Dialpad** are included in online meetings, they can identify in real time when a customer raises a particular objection or mentions a competitor—and then prompt the seller with the relevant talking points, battle card, or sales tactic they should be using on a popup screen visible only to them.

Without AI tools, this type of coaching has typically been done during ride-along sales calls with other sellers or managers, who all have other items competing for time on their calendars. The ability of AI coaches to be part of every call, with every seller, in every deal can have a massive impact on seller skill development.

Deployment of virtual coaches requires a lot of work on the "people and culture" focus for AI readiness, though. When employees feel that their leadership is watching, transcribing, and scoring every moment of every interaction they have on the job, it can be easy to feel that an Orwellian surveillance culture has taken hold. And if AI data is only used for correction and never reward—or if it influences termination decisions—employers may quickly find their teams questioning whether the legal grounds for a hostile work environment have been established.

Your governance and ethics council will want to think carefully about how to ensure that the tools are used as developmental tools rather than evaluative ones to frame their use appropriately. Perhaps managers or sales enablement teams are only given access to team-wide summaries of development needs, while seller-specific details are restricted to the individual seller they pertain to.

POST-MEETING AUTOMATION

After a call has concluded, frontline sellers can gain a lot of time and efficiency by using AI tools to assist with a variety of follow-up tasks—including meeting summaries, action item tracking, and future meeting planning.

Level 1: Foundational

In addition to in-call transcription tools, there are a variety of AI bots that can join calls and then send the seller a follow-up note with the full audio/video recording, a searchable transcript, and an AI-generated summary of key topics and action items.

As of this writing, products like **Fireflies.ai, Read.ai,** and **Otter.ai** all offer licensing options for individual sellers—often with a free-to-use version for a limited period of time or number of calls.

Level 2: Advanced

At the broader team level, tools like **Gong, Outreach**'s Kaia, and **ZoomInfo**'s **Chorus.ai** provide deeper analysis of conversations—identifying ratios of talking vs. listening by the seller, how many questions were asked, and even measures of the customer's sentiment at different points in the conversation.

From the collection of recordings, trends can be identified—leaders can search across all calls to identify mentions of a new competitor, or grab snippets of calls to incorporate into training "best practices" on topics like objection handling.

Level 3: AI-Enabled

At the highest level of maturity, AI systems don't just analyze the conversations; they automatically execute the next steps in the sales process based on what was discussed.

When the tool has access to information about your preferred sales methodology, it can also answer questions like "Who was identified as the champion?" or "Have we identified the budget holder?"—and then automatically update the appropriate MEDDIC fields in your CRM system, change the deal's forecast category, or log critical pain points for inclusion in future demos and proposals. Similarly, an agent might use this information to draft a highly personalized follow-up email that references the specific topics and action items from the call.

Case Study: A Faster Product Launch With Conversational Intelligence

The Challenge

A company that provides solutions for field sales and service was worried about the potential effects COVID-19 would have on its demand. In the first three weeks of the pandemic, they built a new product suited for their customers' "work from home" mandates—but the compressed launch timeline meant little market testing took place before bringing it to market.

Additionally, the company had just implemented its own transition away from a traditional sales floor where leadership would normally overhear live calls to coach sellers on the new, unproven messaging and adapt to emerging objections.

The Solution: The Digital Sales Floor & Curation Engine

The company leveraged a conversational intelligence platform to act as a "digital sales floor," allowing leadership to inspect and scale winning behaviors in real time.

- **Accelerated market monitoring:** Leadership used conversational intelligence tools to gain real-time access to transcripts of every call conducted—many more than they'd been listening to in person. This allowed them to immediately identify emerging patterns in customer objections and market sentiment toward the new product.

- **Curation of "hero moments":** Managers identified 30- to 60-second "gold standard" snippets in which a seller successfully navigated a new objection or articulated a specific value proposition that resonated.

- **Peer-to-Peer knowledge sharing:** These curated clips were broadcast to the full 175-person sales team, helping them to iterate on the pitch daily, informed by the experiences of the entire team.

The ROI

- **21-day proficiency ramp:** The entire sales organization achieved proficiency in a brand-new product category within three weeks, while working entirely in a distributed, remote environment.

- **Unified messaging at scale:** The "telephone game" effect—where messaging degrades as it passes through a large team—was eliminated, ensuring 100% alignment on the new market position.

- **Revenue resilience:** Despite the challenges facing its primary industry, the company successfully scaled the new product to become a primary growth driver, maintaining—and even improving—its revenue trajectory through a tumultuous time.

Because these updates and communications impact your forecast and pipeline assessment with significant real-world implications, you might ultimately decide to have the agent's work stop at the point where it has queued up a set of proposed updates or email messages, which a sales professional reviews and provides a final "human touch" to before hitting send.

Being successful at this requires an organizational commitment to robust, highly integrated tech systems and a high level of trust in the AI's ability to correctly interpret conversations and update critical systems of record. It is also the clear direction major enterprise platforms, such as **Clari, Outreach,** and **Salesloft,** are moving toward.

As companies increasingly use AI tools to automate the routine work of entry-level sellers in Level 2 and 3 applications, there has been increasing concern about whether they are actively deskilling our workforces.

For example, if an AI agent always responds to the customer's technical questions before giving the seller a chance to do it themselves—or if a tool is always prompting an entry-level seller with the best next steps in their deal—the seller may never develop the critical thinking skills or experience to be able to handle these situations on their own.

Because those skills serve as the foundation for the work done by higher-level professionals in the organization, a company that outsources too much entry-level work to AI tools may find that it no longer has a bench of up-and-coming talent with the knowledge, skills, or experience needed to be ready for higher-level jobs.

You'll want to spend time thinking about how workers will develop more value-adding skills as part of your strategic vision and business alignment assessment of your AI projects with these examples in mind, as well as what the new "table stakes skills" are for your entry-level sellers.

IN SUM

The ability to capture, structure, and analyze conversational data is perhaps the most profound change AI is bringing to the frontline seller. For the first time, their spoken conversation—historically the most valuable but least accessible intelligence in the entire go-to-market motion—is being transformed into a structured, searchable, analyzable asset.

From the first moments of morning planning to the final follow-up email of the day, sellers can use AI tools to automate low-value-adding tasks, identify critical insights, and amplify their effectiveness. By delegating the rote work of data entry, research, and administration to their new lowest-cost resource, the seller frees themselves to focus on the uniquely human, high-value work of communicating, connecting, and selling.

This change, however, requires a rethinking of the skills needed to succeed as a seller. No longer is the ability to manually execute a high volume of tasks (like making 100 dials or sending 200 generic emails) the mark of a top performer. Instead, their value lies in their ability to think strategically and to act as an orchestrator of these powerful new tools to enable even more personalized, human-to-human conversations.

The modern seller needs to know which AI systems to engage when, how to prompt them to create the perfect response, and how to interpret the AI-generated insights in a way that improves and informs their human-led decisions.

Becoming an AI-enabled seller won't happen overnight. Starting small, by choosing an area of the daily workflow that can be addressed with a Level 1 solution, is a great idea—whether that's taking meeting notes or finding contact information for a prospect list.

Building on small wins, sellers (and their organizations) can build the momentum and confidence to explore more advanced applications and make bigger-ticket, team-wide investments.

This table summarizes the tactical applications discussed in this chapter. Use it as a quick reference guide to assess the state of your current processes, identify the next logical step in your AI journey, and create a starting list of vendors to explore for your own tech stack.

Process Stage	Specific Task	AI Application	Example Vendors/Products
Planning & Prioritization	Prioritizing which leads/ opportunities to work on	Predictive Lead & Opportunity Scoring	Salesforce Einstein, HubSpot Sales Hub, Clari, Gong, Outreach, Salesloft
	Identifying accounts that are actively in-market	Buyer Intent Data Analysis	6sense, ZoomInfo, Cognism, Bombora
Prospecting	Finding verified contact data (email, phone)	AI Data Enrichment & Verification	Wiza, Rocket Reach, Apollo.io, Seamless.AI, ZoomInfo, Cognism
	Researching accounts and contacts for personalization	Automated Account & Persona Research	Clay, Cognism (Cortex AI), ZoomInfo (Copilot)
Outreach & Engagement	Improving the quality and tone of individual emails	Real-Time Email Coaching	Gemini, ChatGPT, Lavender, HubSpot AI Assistant, Regie.ai
	Writing multistep, multichannel outreach campaigns	Generative AI Sequence Creation	Outreach, Salesloft, Regie.ai, Reply.io
	Managing initial prospect replies and questions	Autonomous AI Response Handling	Reply.io (Jason AI), 6sense (AI Email Agents), Lindy.ai, Qualified (PiperX)

Process Stage	Specific Task	AI Application	Example Vendors/Products
Meeting Intelligence	Preparing for an upcoming sales meeting	Automated Pre-Meeting Briefing Generation	ChatGPT, Outreach (Smart Account Assist), Cirrus Insight (Meeting AI)
	Handling objections and questions during a live call	Real-Time In-Meeting Coaching & Battle Cards	Gong, Outreach (Kaia), Clari (Copilot), Avoma, Dialpad
Post-Meeting Admin	Taking notes and capturing action items	AI Transcription & Meeting Summarization	Fireflies.ai, Read.ai, Otter.ai, Microsoft Teams, Zoom, Google Meet
	Analyzing call effectiveness for coaching	Conversational Intelligence & Analysis	Gong, Outreach (Kaia), ZoomInfo (Chorus.ai)
	Updating CRM and drafting follow-up emails	Automated CRM Data Entry & Follow-up Generation	Clari, Outreach, Salesloft

AI FOR SALES ENGINEERS

In complex B2B sales environments—especially SaaS software, telecommunications, and manufacturing—the sales engineer (also known as the solutions consultant or pre-sales engineer) is often a critical player in achieving the technical win. Yet staffing models are often unbalanced—with a single SE supporting between four and eight quota-carrying account executives.

This resource scarcity can often create a critical bottleneck where customers need to wait days or weeks to get a demonstration from a qualified technical engineer, unnecessarily elongating the sales cycle. AI tools have emerged as a powerful way to relieve this pressure.

DEMO CUSTOMIZATION

Level 1: Foundational

In many organizations, stretched SE talent has developed a standard "harbor tour" demonstration of their platform. Lacking the time to accompany their account executives on every discovery call, the SE takes prospects through an initial, generic demonstration that covers the major features of the product and then conducts a deeper dive "on the fly" when the prospect shows interest.

Not only is it an inefficient use of high-paid technical talent's time to conduct the same repetitive presentation over and over, but it also misses an opportunity to clearly connect a buyer's pain points with product solutions. Prospects are often forced to sit through demonstration components that are irrelevant to their business problem—which may introduce unnecessary objections or questions into the sales cycle—while the truly deal-moving topics get short shrift.

In the same way that a frontline seller may use an LLM like ChatGPT, Claude, or Gemini to conduct pre-meeting prep, sales engineers can use similar tools—seeded with a library of demo content, product specs, and notes from any discovery calls that have already taken place without them—to create a custom demo script for every interaction in minutes.

Your governance council will want to weigh in on specific tools for use in this process, ensuring that confidential or proprietary information doesn't get used to train public LLMs in the process—but this is a simple first use of AI that can pay large dividends.

Level 2: Advanced

In a more advanced use case, a series of AI-driven demo automation platforms have emerged that allow SEs to offer prospects the opportunity to explore early demo environments independently—deferring this basic task to an AI-based environment and saving their own time for more complicated demos with higher-intent buyers.

Unlike the on-demand access to prerecorded demos that many organizations have implemented to scale their SE teams' impact, these tools offer interactive product sandboxes that use AI to personalize the flow based on the prospect's role and real-time engagement.

Generative AI is increasingly used in these environments to auto-personalize content—replacing generic placeholders like "ACME Corp" with the prospect's company name, logos, and industry-specific data without manual work.

Case Study: Accelerating International SE Onboarding via AI-Guided Scripting

The Challenge

A B2B SaaS company with €15M in annual revenue faced a major scaling bottleneck when it expanded from its legacy presence in Europe to start serving the US market.

Historically, they relied on a small group of highly tenured sellers and a single European sales engineer (with deep, tribal knowledge of the product) to deliver demos. Consequently, US-based demos could only be scheduled during early morning hours to accommodate the European SE's time zone.

The Solution

To decentralize expertise and speed up US operations, the company developed a proprietary AI sales assistant specialized in technical sales execution. This domain-specific AI model was trained on three core pillars: complete product technical documentation, the official company sales playbook (including a specific demo framework), and verbatim scripts from high-performing product tour recordings.

Before a call, a new SE would consult the AI agent, providing the prospect's website and any identified pain points. The AI would synthesize recent news headlines and discovery notes to generate a custom-tailored demo script.

The ROI

- **Reduced time-to-value:** The new US-based SE led independent, high-quality demos within just four months of hire.
- **Operational agility:** The company eliminated time zone restrictions, allowing it to offer demo slots during standard US business hours without relying on the European team.

> - **Methodology consistency:** By leveraging the AI's training on proven sales frameworks, the company ensured that even new hires delivered demos that were more focused and strategic than those of previous "shadow-trained" recruits.
> - **Cost savings:** The firm significantly reduced the need for international travel and the opportunity cost of taking tenured SEs from their own territories to train new hires.

The strategic implication for the sales engineer is a shift in their earliest engagement with prospects. By offering a basic demo experience before their first meeting, the SE enters their first live call knowing exactly which features the prospect hovered over, clicked on, or rewatched. This allows them to skip the introductory presentation and focus immediately on complex, tailored solutioning for the highest-intent prospects.

Vendors like **Navattic** specialize in no-code, interactive demos that can be embedded directly, and **Reprise** emphasizes the ability of "perfect" sandbox environments to avoid bugs, user conflict, or data inconsistencies that often plague live demo environments, ensuring that a technical glitch never derails the sales narrative.

Players in this space also argue that the demo serves as a mechanism for tracking buyer persona activities and personalizing engagement. **Demoboost** uses AI to not only clone the software environment but to generate narrative voiceovers and text guides based on the persona of the viewer (so that a CFO sees a finance-centric narrative while a CTO sees an architecture-centric one).

Meanwhile, **Consensus** emphasizes how easy these demos are to share on websites or send via email—alongside the ability to track when they've been shared with unidentified stakeholders who nevertheless will influence the ultimate buying decision.

RFP MANAGEMENT

The sales engineering team is also often a major player in responding to customer RFPs, which can take days or hours to complete. In doing so, SEs find themselves responding to many of the same questions repeatedly ("Does your system provide five nines of uptime?" "Can you provide your most recent SOC2 report?").

Level 2: Advanced

To facilitate these processes, specialized platforms such as **AutoRFP. ai** and **Tenderbolt** ingest customer RFPs and map them to a library of approved content to create a "first pass" response in minutes. While vendors like **Loopio** emphasize that their solutions focus heavily on content freshness, your sales engineer will want to validate that the result is current and appropriate for the customer situation—especially since they are part of the sales team that will ultimately be held responsible for ensuring the product that is implemented works as promised.

IN SUM

The sales engineer has traditionally been the scarce resource of the GTM organization, often stretched thin across multiple account executives and forced into a cycle of repetitive, generic demonstrations. By delegating the rote work of demo preparation and initial RFP drafting to AI, the SE can move from being a tactical bottleneck to a strategic accelerator of the technical win.

Here is a summary of the AI applications discussed for sales engineers.

Process Stage	Specific Task	AI Application	Example Vendors/Products
Demo Customization	Creating tailored demo scripts	Seed LLMs with product specs and discovery notes to create custom demo scripts	ChatGPT, Claude, Gemini
	Provide interactive, self-service demos	Personalized product tours that adapt to the prospect's role and engagement	Navattic, Reprise, Demoboost
	Tracking buyer intent	Track feature-level engagement	Navattic, Consensus
RFP Management	Respond to technical RFPs	Create "first pass" responses from approved libraries	AutoRFP.ai, Tenderbolt, Loopio

AI FOR THE FRONTLINE MANAGER

Within the go-to-market organization, the frontline sales manager is perhaps one of the most difficult, high-pressure roles. Situated at the bridge between salespeople and the executive leadership team, they are expected to participate in complex management and leadership decisions while also being in the trenches, helping their salespeople sell.

Many frontline managers were top-performing sellers themselves. They earned a promotion into leadership as a result, even though the skills required to succeed are fundamentally different.

A great seller thrives on individual achievement, personal quota attainment, and competition. In contrast, a great manager must prioritize predictability, consistency, and the collaborative development of a team in which everyone contributes to the result.

Without great training to move into the role, many first-time managers struggle to shift their mindset from "me" to "we"—and, as a result, jump in as a super-seller to close their team's deals by themselves at the first sign of trouble. This approach disempowers sellers and stifles their development—creating a cycle of dependency that requires even more super-selling by their ever-extended manager.

Ultimately, the manager becomes a bottleneck to team performance, limiting the team's revenue potential to their own personal span of control and stalling their own career in the process.

Equipping frontline managers with AI tools can help them move past this common trap. If 72% of an individual contributor's time is spent on nonselling tasks, their manager carries an even greater administrative burden—robbing their calendar of time spent on uniquely human, high-impact activities like strategic thinking, motivational leadership, and personalized development coaching.

This chapter focuses on practical applications of AI that can empower the frontline manager to spend more time on the activities that truly drive their team's performance.

COACHING

At the top of the frontline manager's list of responsibilities is coaching, yet it often falls by the wayside as the constant drumbeat to close the next deal demands their time.

As sales teams become increasingly remote, there are fewer opportunities for ad hoc, serendipitous interaction, further limiting the coaching sellers receive from their direct manager. As a result, much of the coaching comes in the form of generic advice delivered on all-team calls, which lack the personalization needed by a team with diverse skill sets, personalities, and motivations.

Even managers who are strongly committed to creating time for individualized coaching run into challenges with scale and objectivity. It's simply not possible for a manager to be on every call or participate in every meeting—and the feedback they can give is often based on anecdotal evidence or gut feel from limited interaction. Managers find it easy to identify the extreme ends of the performance curve—the sellers who are clearly superior or woefully deficient—but the majority in the middle often lose out on necessary coaching that can move them into the top-performing categories.

THE VIRTUAL GAME TAPE ROOM

As tools like **Gong, Chorus.ai, Avoma,** or **Dialpad** increasingly join every online meeting, they automatically create a searchable "game tape room" for the entire sales team. These tools can automatically record, transcribe, and analyze every sales call and video meeting, allowing the manager to see exactly what was said, how it was received, and, ideally, suggest opportunities for improvement.

Level 1: Foundational

At the foundational level, these tools can provide conversational intelligence measures of basic communication skills. Talk-to-listen ratios and flagging the longest monologue can warn sellers that they're dominating calls or lecturing instead of listening, while a measure of the number and type of questions can help assess the quality of their discovery processes.

Sentiment analysis and topic tracking can also help identify recurring themes or responses sellers elicit from their customers—creating a great jumping-off point for coaching discussions about real-world performance.

Managers will want to tread carefully and seek guidance from their governance council to ensure their use of technology doesn't cross any legal or ethical lines.

When AI tools score calls, they use natural language processing to draw conclusions about sentiment and key points. Yet research has consistently shown that some standard speech-to-text and sentiment analysis models perform more poorly on non-native English speakers, female voices, and diverse accents—rating these speakers as less "authoritative" or "confident" than their white male counterparts.

To avoid inadvertently engaging in illegal discrimination, your governance framework might dictate that conversational tools' advice should be seen as "hypotheses to investigate" instead of "conclusions that have been reached" and should never be used for performance reviews or formal performance improvement plans unless the frontline manager has listened to the complete recording of the call themselves and drawn their own independent conclusion.

Level 2: Advanced

Spotlighting Team-Wide Trends

When CI tools have been augmented with a company's sales playbook, they can search for trends across multiple sellers and calls—shaping the agenda for the team's group development.

If, for example, a company is using the MEDDPICC framework, analysis of the call recordings from the manager's team might show that there is an across-the-board lack of questioning around the economic buyer in deals, suggesting that a refresher training session on the topic might be appropriate for the next team call.

When completed, the manager might run a bit of a competition—telling their team that they're emphasizing this skill for the next month, and asking team members to flag call recordings where they do a particularly good job of probing on the economic buyer's identity. The seller with the best example might win a gift card, and the recording of their call can be pulled into official training materials as a "best practice" for the team to emulate—or it might be shared for company-wide use.

These use cases will require sign-off by your legal team, who needs to determine whether the prospects (and the sellers) have consented to their call recording being used in this way. Calls might start with a warning that they are being recorded "for training and quality assurance purposes," but that may not necessarily mean those recordings can be used as permanent marketing or training assets. In jurisdictions such as Illinois (BIPA) and the European Union (GDPR), such uses may incur legal liability.

Automated Call Scoring and Post-Call Analysis

With the sales playbook in hand, AI tools can also automatically evaluate every call against a predefined scorecard—grading sellers on their adherence to the sales methodology, objection handling, or definition of next steps. AI tools might also provide recommended next steps when they're absent and share all of this analysis with the seller or manager, who can now effectively review a 60-minute meeting in just five minutes, spending more time on actual coaching rather than searching for coachable moments.

Level 3: AI-Enabled

To be successful, these kinds of development programs have to come with a cultural understanding that such micro-analysis of their calls isn't a "big brother" management style—it's a foundation for truly personalized development. The frontline manager is one of the key carriers of culture in the sales organization—and your readiness assessment will need to equip them to speak effectively about these real concerns.

When the culture is receptive to it, truly AI-enabled organizations can diagnose patterns across time and automatically prescribe targeted coaching plans.

For example, a model might indicate that a particular seller consistently struggles with pricing objections, while their colleague fails to secure concrete next steps. With these insights, the first seller might be assigned a micro-learning module on value-based selling, while the second might be given a role-playing simulation to complete at any time or place that's convenient to them.

For these use cases, your governance council will want legal advice on whether training suggestions constitute "automated employment decisions," and might consider demanding that a frontline manager fill the role of human overseer who reviews AI suggestions and validates recommended development plans before they're given to an employee. Without doing so, you risk creating a "black box" performance assessment that would be difficult or impossible to defend in a legal challenge.

DEAL REVIEWS

Frontline managers are often available to provide coaching for ad hoc reasons—they happened to be available when a call was happening, a seller mentioned a particular challenge they were having, or some other serendipitous circumstance. Yet many GTM organizations also have a formalized "deal review" process that provides coaching for opportunities of specific importance—those that are a particular size, have reached a specific stage, or involve a high-impact prospect.

Sometimes, these deal reviews take on an unstructured format: the seller meets with their manager and a few other colleagues who are especially interested in the deal—they share what they've done, and the group shares their ideas on how to increase the odds of winning.

In more advanced organizations, a particular sales framework—such as BANT, MEDDIC, or SPIN—provides a series of topics to explore in the review, and the session assesses whether the appropriate qualification elements are in place to indicate the deal is on the right track.

While these meetings do provide value, they're traditionally a process of *inspection* rather than one of *intelligence*. They rely more on a seller's subjective narrative, backward-looking data, and human intuition than they do on science to prescribe a path forward.

Level 1: Foundational

By ingesting your deal framework and applying it to transcripts of calls, emails, and CRM data about the opportunity, AI tools can eliminate the messiness of these types of deal reviews, conduct them more often, and provide deal-changing insights as a result.

The process is simple. Before a deal review, the seller shares AI-generated summaries and full transcripts of their calls from tools such as **Zoom, Microsoft Teams, Fireflies.ai,** or **Otter.ai.**

Combining them with their documented sales framework—or even just relying on the fact that LLMs like **Gemini** or **ChatGPT** are familiar with their general principles—can be enough foundation for a prompt that will summarize the strengths and weaknesses of an opportunity in a report to be delivered to participants before the deal review meeting even happens.

You'll want to be sure, of course, that you're not sharing confidential or proprietary information with public AI models—and your governance council can provide guidance on appropriate tools to use for this sort of analysis. You'll also want to be sure that your AI tools are analyzing data that is a representative sample of the entire deal history—rather than just a curated selection of the seller's best moments—to get useful advice.

Level 2: Advanced

Going a step further, an organization that has deployed a comprehensive revenue intelligence platform like **Clari, Outreach,** or **Salesloft** might query those systems for a data-driven health score on the deal, with key risk factors flagged—which can guide the group's thinking on the best next steps to improve the score.

Level 3: AI-Enabled

For the fully AI-enabled organization, frontline managers may not have to wait for a predefined schedule or size trigger to prompt the need for a clinic—the AI tool might flag an opportunity and schedule the call because it has noticed negative signals like a key champion's job change announced on LinkedIn, a lack of communication on next steps, or some other indicator.

Moreover, an integrated AI system might create prescriptive, data-driven recommendations for the team to consider as the best next steps, based on patterns of activity it has identified in highly similar deals.

For example, the recommendation might sound like "For luxury retail prospects of this size, winning opportunities have involved having

Case Study: Rescuing At-Risk Revenue via Automated Deal Inspection

The Challenge

A global enterprise provider of solutions for the hospitality industry struggled with deals that appeared healthy in the CRM but ultimately stalled or slipped.

The Solution: Algorithmic Deal Health Monitoring

The organization implemented a revenue intelligence platform to move from subjective reporting to automated deal inspection. By analyzing historical win patterns in "similar other opportunities," the system provided an objective "health score" for every opportunity in the pipeline.

- **Automated risk flagging:** The platform's AI continuously scanned communication velocity and buyer engagement. It proactively flagged high-value deals where engagement had dropped below the "success baseline," alerting both the seller and management before the deal reached a point of no return.

- **Diagnosis of "the why":** Rather than just identifying a low probability of closing, the system provided specific diagnostic reasons. Common flags included a lack of **multithreading** (identifying that no executive-level or technical stakeholders were involved) and the absence of a **mutual action plan** (confirming that no documented agreement on next steps had been shared with the prospect).

- **Leadership intervention:** Managers used these AI-generated insights to conduct "deal clinics," focusing specifically on the gaps identified by the software—such as ghosting champions or missing procurement milestones.

The ROI

- **Rescuing "slipped" deals:** By intervening early in the "at-risk" deals flagged by the AI tool, the company saw a significant reduction in

> slipped revenue, contributing to a **70% year-over-year growth in bookings.**
>
> - **Shortened sales cycles:** The transition to a data-driven **mutual action plan** ensured that both the buyer and seller stayed aligned on deadlines, reducing the friction that typically extends enterprise sales cycles.
>
> - **Forecast integrity:** Moving away from anecdotal updates to data-backed inspection allowed the company to achieve 95% or greater forecast accuracy, as "at-risk" deals were either rescued or purged from the pipeline far earlier in the quarter.

one of the implementation team members who worked on the Coach account conduct a needs assessment workshop."

The human experts—the seller, the manager, and others involved in the deal review—can then use their knowledge of the specific relationships and political landscape within their account to contextualize, refine, and execute the AI's data-driven suggestion.

This use case is an increasing focus for all major revenue intelligence platforms—but a human expert remains the best final filter to determine whether their data-driven suggestions are appropriate for real-world use.

TERRITORY MANAGEMENT AND QBRS

While many frontline managers might struggle to find the time for individual-level coaching at the frequency they'd prefer, they're still often able to organize a team-wide QBR every 90 days. In them, sellers are told to "think like a business owner of their own territory franchise," and prepare a deck to be shared at a team meeting that highlights what's been going well, what's been challenging, which accounts are priorities for the next quarter, and what the most likely path to quota achievement is.

If our guiding principle for AI-based tools is to delegate work to the lowest-cost resource capable of doing the most time-consuming tasks, a great candidate for automation is this QBR deck preparation. Collecting data, recalling performance detail, and writing narratives are not high-level sales strategy tasks—they're an administrative burden that often precedes thoughtful, accurate, and objective analysis of territory performance, making them ripe for AI automation.

Level 1: Foundational

Generative AI tools can serve as powerful assistance in the deck-creation process, generating the first draft of QBR materials in minutes. By providing them key CRM reports or BI dashboards, sellers can prompt LLMs with natural language requests like "Build a QBR deck with this template to summarize the health of the Chicago region—with key emphasis on quota achievement, pipeline coverage for the next 90 days, and key customer relationships."

AppEQ (Smart Slides), **Matik**, and **Rollstack** are solutions designed specifically for PowerPoint deck generation, integrating with CRM tools such as Salesforce and HubSpot to assemble slides using predefined templates.

Even general-purpose presentation AI tools can be a valuable starting point. Sellers who use **Gemini** in Slides, **Beautiful.ai,** or **Canva's Magic Design** can combine simple text prompts with existing documents (like a territory plan) to generate a polished, visually appealing presentation draft. This allows the seller to focus their energy on refining the narrative and adding strategic context—they gain time to think that would previously be spent wrestling with formatting and data entry.

Level 2: Advanced

When sellers produce QBR materials more quickly, the additional time saved can also be used to increase collaboration with their frontline manager on the insights they provide.

Case Study: Automating Internal Territory Health Reviews

The Challenge

A fast-growing insurance technology division struggled with significant "reporting overhead" during internal account and territory review—individual contributors were spending over 30 minutes preparing for manager meetings every two weeks.

Because the preparation required information from CRM, BI tools, and internal product databases, internal meetings often devolved into fact-finding missions with the majority of the managers and AEs' time together spent verifying the data and "reporting the news" rather than discussing strategy or identifying growth opportunities.

The Solution: Automated Data Storytelling

The organization used an AI platform to populate a territory-specific health-check template with a simple "one-click" process.

- **Dynamic template integration:** The AI templates connect directly to the team's live data sources, allowing them to select a specific account or territory and generate a complete, data-driven presentation or one-pager instantly.

- **Unified data visualization:** The platform automatically pulled and visualized key performance indicators—such as product usage trends, support ticket volume, and renewal risk—ensuring that a consistent "story" was given to leadership.

- **From data gathering to strategic coaching:** By automating the "what" (the data), the organization shifted the focus of internal meetings to the "so what" (the strategy).

The ROI

- **93% reduction in preparation time:** Individual prep time for internal reviews dropped from over 30 minutes to under two minutes per account.

> - **2,700 hours saved annually:** Across the entire organization, the team reclaimed thousands of hours of productivity per year. This time was reallocated from administrative copy-pasting to proactive, customer-facing activities.
> - **Improved decision velocity:** Leadership gained a real-time, accurate view of territory health across the entire division. This eliminated the "data lag" common in manual reporting and ensured that interventions in at-risk accounts happened weeks earlier than they would have under the previous manual system.

Tools like **Clari** inform the conversation with the risks present in any individual deal included in the territory plan, while functionality from **Outreach** and **HubSpot Sales Hub** can help generate a list of prioritized accounts for the next quarter by predicting which leads are most likely to convert.

Newer tools like **Pocus** focus on creating narrative explanations for why an account might be a priority, highlighting multithreaded interest in the account, recent executive changes in the news, and recent website visits as reasons to pay attention to them.

Here, too, AI tools can become an active intelligence partner that informs QBR conversations—often with deep predictive insights.

Level 3: AI-Enabled

At the most integrated level, AI agents might be deployed to help a seller and manager design a territory strategy by running simulations on a variety of scenarios. As computing power increases and data access becomes easier, we can imagine an environment where a seller or their manager asks strategy questions like "What would happen if I shifted 20% of my time from prospecting in the dense city center of my territory to ABM motions in these five large rural accounts?"

The agents could then play out the scenarios thousands of times and provide a probabilistic assessment of the results—enabling a seller to replace their intuition- and experience-based territory plan with one supported through data-driven simulations. To achieve this goal, however, a highly sophisticated, clean set of data needs to be available for modelling—or the results will be unreliable.

TALENT MANAGEMENT

RELATIONSHIP MANAGEMENT

When I first began managing people, a mentor suggested that I keep a notebook or Word document to track notes from my interactions with each of my direct reports. They were organized as a running log that indicated the date of the conversation, high-level bullet points of what we discussed, next steps, verbatim quotes of directives or feedback I provided, and other related content.

Over the years, I've built hundreds of these documents. They've helped me remember the specifics of each seller's experience (was it the CIO or CTO that they've been trying to connect with in that deal?), and they also provide a timeline to see the progression of issues from small observations, through notable development opportunities, to focused training and skills mastery.

When employee separations have become contentious, these logs have also been invaluable pieces of evidence that my HR and legal teams have used to resolve them quickly.

AI tools provide the opportunity to automate the mundane task of "documenting what we discussed," freeing up time and attention for the more important (and human-centered) discussions about "What's next and how can I help?"

Level 1: Foundational

An easy first step is to delegate the notetaking task to an AI meeting assistant who can automatically join, record, transcribe, and summarize each 1:1. This allows the manager and the seller to be fully present and engaged with one another in the conversation, knowing that they'll receive a summary of key discussion points and action items after the meeting is concluded.

For online 1:1s, this functionality is increasingly becoming standard in the meeting software itself—such as **Zoom AI Companion**—or through plugin tools like **Fathom** or **Otter.ai,** which can look for meetings on your Microsoft calendar and join any **Teams** meetings it finds.

Level 2: Advanced

With reliable note-taking in place, 1:1s can become more strategic when the frontline manager uses AI as a forward-looking planner. In this use case, an AI assistant integrates with your CRM system and reviews notes from previous meetings to proactively suggest agenda items for your discussion—suggesting the manager review a particular opportunity that has been stalled in the contract approval stage for two weeks, or reminding them to follow up on the seller's professional development goals. Tools like **Fellow** and **ClickUp** offer meeting agenda-setting functionality, with varying levels of integrations to the wider sales tech stack.

Level 3: AI-Enabled

In the future, frontline managers in fully enabled organizations might find that these systems are completely integrated into daily workflows so that they set agendas proactively.

Seeing that I've got a 1:1 scheduled with John, an agent might look through call recordings, CRM updates, and other tools to create an "intelligence briefing" for me with insights like "John's talk-to-listen ratio on his discovery calls was 62:38, which is significantly above the team average of 42:58. This is a key coaching topic to address. At the same time, he leads the team in the number of times he's used the new messaging to introduce your latest product release—recognize and reward this behavior."

At this level of enablement, however, we can't forget the importance that human judgment plays in the talent development process. If the manager allows the 1:1 meeting to devolve into a situation where they simply read an AI tool's assessments and suggestions to the seller, they've eliminated their own value—and destroyed a "safe space" for real development to occur.

ASSESSMENT

For a seller promoted to their first management role, talent assessment is one of the key new skills they need to learn. Hopefully, they've received detailed performance reviews through the course of their career and know what they're supposed to look like—but these conversations still may feel foreign when they're the deliverer of the review.

Moreover, the seller who has been promoted into management likely had a string of top-ranked reviews—their time in management may be the first time they see what a review looks like for a seller who needs improvement or ultimately needs to be exited from the organization.

AI tools can assist the talent review process in a number of ways.

Level 1: Foundational

The most immediate application is to help managers draft the review itself using generative AI tools. A well-structured, professional narrative can be created in moments when a prompt includes a copy of the job description, the manager's notes from 1:1s, and some additional bullet points on the seller's achievements, challenges, and goals for the next quarter.

The manager can provide additional prompts ("make it more formal," "structure all goals with the SMART framework," or "provide more encouragement," for example) or suggest the categories that may exist on a standard HR template ("Please make the first section a review of sales metrics, then a review of each of the skills in the job description, then a final section on professional development goals to support them in their desire to the next job promotion").

By using AI to generate a comprehensive first draft, the manager can save time on basic composition and spend their time refining the message, adding relevant context, and supplying additional detail that only a person who interacts with the seller can provide.

Level 2: Advanced

Beyond basic writing assistance, the next level of maturity uses AI to compile and analyze underlying performance data, creating an objective foundation for the review. Here, the AI platform acts as a central data synthesizer, bringing in details from the CRM tool, conversational intelligence platform, activity metrics from sales automation tools, and narratives collected from 360-degree peer review surveys.

The systems that sellers interact with each day—such as **Gong, Clari,** and **Salesforce**—are key sources to draw on, and HR platforms like **Betterworks, Lattice,** and **PerformYard** use AI to summarize themes from 360 feedback, track development milestones, or create data-backed insights for inclusion in the review.

No matter how well intentioned, human managers are susceptible to errors in judgment—particularly recency bias (where they overemphasize performance observations from the past few weeks of interaction) and personal affinity bias (where they unconsciously favor sellers that they personally like). The introduction of AI tools to the performance process can help counter these biases—as long as the data they've been trained on doesn't introduce biases of their own.

At the same time, using AI tools for performance evaluation may introduce a lot of legal, ethical, and cultural risks to an organization, and your governance council will want to spend a lot of time thinking through the nuances of these use cases.

Because AI tools make decisions based on the data they've been trained on, they potentially codify bad habits that the organization might not want. If, for example, flawed human leaders historically reviewed sellers who came from a different race, gender identity, or socioeconomic class than their own as "low performers," an AI tool trained on their data might potentially create discriminatory evaluations at scale, without revealing too much about how it arrived at its results.

This "black box" of decision-making around all sorts of employment issues will be unpacked more fully in the chapter devoted to legal and ethical considerations for sales, but talent management is perhaps the single highest-risk area for your governance, ethics, and legal teams to evaluate due to strict employment laws that vary in different geographies.

Level 3: AI-Enabled

If used appropriately, however, AI in these use cases can improve the quarterly or annual performance review process that many managers find cumbersome. Looking to the future, we can envision a world where AI agents assist in a *continuous* process of performance review and prediction—gleaning insights in real-time as employees send emails, engage in sales calls, or participate in internal meetings—adding these examples and recommendations to an "always live" coaching document that the seller and manager have access to and review as part of their weekly 1:1s or daily interaction.

Such a framework can also help the manager and seller move beyond the task of "reviewing past performance" and focus instead on future potential—prescribing optimal development paths to get there.

To make this vision a reality, the organization's machine learning model must be trained on its historical data to correlate specific skills and behaviors with business outcomes—and all constituencies must have a high level of trust that the models being used are accurate, unbiased, and effective in developing talent across time.

RECRUITING

The frontline manager is not just a developer of talent, however. They also have a responsibility to build stronger teams by recruiting new team members—and many first-time managers conduct candidate interviews that are disconnected from the written job description, which is often just "something pulled from a file" to post online. The result is that a lot of "conversations" happen in interviews, but not a lot of "assessment on real ability to succeed in the job."

AI can help managers recruit great talent by crafting a clear, precise definition of what "good" looks like for each role and building an interview process that separates the "good" from the "great." Here, too, your governance council will want to play a very active role in ensuring that your use of AI meets all of the legal and ethical obligations you have as employers in the geographies you work in.

SOURCING

Level 1: Foundational

At the foundational level, a manager can begin by using a generative AI tool of their choice to craft a compelling job description to recruit against. Prompt the tool to ask you for the outcomes you're seeking, along with the core competencies required to get there.

It might take some iteration, but the goal is not just to identify the quota and territory—you want to highlight the specific factors that will allow a seller to succeed in your specific context.

For example, you might provide a prompt like: "Draft a job description for an enterprise account executive in the Dallas area. The key objective is to achieve a $1.2M annual quota by closing 10 new logo deals. Key competencies include: managing a complex, consultative sales process; the ability to disrupt customer thinking; and self-sufficiently generating 70% of their own pipeline."

By continuing to use the AI tool as a conversational partner in the draft, you might ask **Claude, ChatGPT, Gemini,** or others to "match my company's 'professional but approachable' brand voice," stay within a certain word count limit, or create sections for legally required disclosures or disclaimers according to your hiring location and industry.

Level 2: Advanced

Specialized platforms like **Grammarly Business** and **Workable** often include pre-built templates and workflows specifically designed for writing hiring content.

Additionally, vendors such as **Textio** and **Datapeople** can compare your job description to datasets from real-world hiring processes to guide targeted changes. Their AI tools can identify keywords that improve search engine optimization, scan for gender- or race-biased language, and even benchmark your expectations against industry standards to ensure you're not chasing a set of qualifications that are unrealistic for the market.

Level 3: AI-Enabled

AI-enabled organizations use agents to proactively scan for hiring information beyond a simple LinkedIn search. They can aggregate information from patent filings, public records, or professional publications to build a multidimensional profile of a candidate's fit for the job—and also scan your applicant tracking system to rediscover talent that might have been a strong contender in a previous search, but hasn't applied for this role (so long as these use cases are complying with the data retention and privacy policies the candidate originally agreed to).

Vendors like **Eightfold.ai, Beamery,** and **SeekOut** offer solutions in this area, and some also incorporate generative AI to create unique outreach messages for every target candidate by sending personalized messages about the role and responding appropriately when candidates reply.

Once AI tools have been used to attract the right candidates, the human manager's job is still to verify the fit. Just as recruiters are using AI to write job postings, candidates are using the same tools to write resumes and applications for them. Without a human in the middle, you run the risk of two algorithms talking to one another, but no real "assessment" taking place.

CANDIDATE MATCHING

Level 1: Foundational

As the frontline manager begins screening candidates for a match to their open position, they can return to their generative AI tool for help in crafting a series of interview questions that are designed to elicit a conversation about each of the "must-have" skills from their job description—as well as a scoring rubric to rank the level of fit.

The following is an example of the output of this exercise for an interview process for a frontline SaaS seller with a $1M quota, living in the US, and reporting to a manager in London. It includes the relevant skills, interview questions, and the screening rubric:

1. TERRITORY PLANNING & EXECUTION

- "Let's imagine you're starting on day one in your new territory. Walk me through your plan for the first 90 days."
- "Tell me about a time you had to build a territory from scratch or turn around an underperforming one. What were the specific steps you took, and what were the results?"
- "How do you decide which accounts to prioritize your time on? Describe your methodology for tiering accounts."

2. COMPLEX DEAL NAVIGATION

- "Walk me through the largest and most complex deal you've closed. Who were the key players on the client's side, and how did you manage those different relationships and priorities?"

- "Describe a time when a deal stalled unexpectedly. What was the cause, how did you diagnose it, and what steps did you take to get it back on track?"
- "How do you gain access to and build relationships with executive-level decision-makers when your initial contact is lower-level?"

3. PROACTIVE & ASYNCHRONOUS COMMUNICATION

- "Tell me about your process for forecasting. How do you ensure your pipeline is accurately reflected in the CRM for a management team in a different time zone?"
- "Describe a situation where you needed critical support from an internal team (like legal or product) that was not readily available. How did you handle the communication and manage the client's expectations?"
- "If you were to send your manager a weekly update email on your territory, what key information and metrics would you include to make it effective?"

4. RESOURCEFULNESS & AUTONOMY

- "Tell me about a time you were given a goal but weren't given the resources or information to achieve it. What did you do?"
- "Describe a professional failure you experienced. What did you learn from it, and what did you change about your process afterward?"
- "How do you stay motivated day-to-day when working remotely without a team physically around you?"

5. BUSINESS ACUMEN

- "Pick a previous client and explain the business case for your solution. How did you calculate the potential ROI, and what metrics did you use?"

- "Describe a time you successfully challenged a prospect's perspective on their own business problem."
- "When you're researching a new key account, what do you look for beyond the names of contacts? What business signals or triggers are most important to you?"

Level 2: Advanced

As AI tools have made it easy for hiring managers to develop and post open positions, they've also made it easier than ever for candidates to submit applications—whether they're qualified or not. As a result, a single job post can garner dozens or hundreds of applications within the first few days of being posted, the vast majority of which are from unqualified applicants.

Overwhelmed managers may simply evaluate the first 10 applications they receive and miss out on the best candidate who got stuck in the middle of the pile. AI tools have the potential to find this needle in the haystack with a timely, fair evaluation of all submitted applications.

Here, too, comprehensive talent intelligence platforms are now using AI-powered systems to interpret the natural language of a resume in the same way a human reader would—inferring skills that aren't explicitly listed in a resume based on the experiences that are (so, a seller who "achieved President's Club in all years on the job" is presumed to have "100% quota attainment"). This is a massive improvement over the strict keyword-matching functionality of older applicant tracking systems.

Level 3: AI-Enabled

Tools like **HireVue** and **Phenom** move organizations into the realm of AI-enabled hiring by providing candidates with one-way video interviews that the candidate can complete on their own time. They draw on a library of standard questions to conduct a structured interview

Skill	1. Does not demonstrate competency	2. Partially demonstrates competency	3. Demonstrates competency	4. Sometimes exceeds competency expectations	5. Far exceeds competency expectations
Territory Planning & Execution	Fails to develop or articulate a territory plan. Is purely reactive, waiting for inbound leads. Shows little understanding of the key accounts or market dynamics in their region.	Creates a basic list of target accounts but lacks a strategic methodology for prioritization or outreach. Prospecting efforts are inconsistent and struggle to build a sufficient pipeline.	Develops and executes a clear, documented territory plan. Consistently applies a methodology to tier accounts and manages time effectively. Reliably builds enough pipeline to meet quota.	Proactively identifies and penetrates new market segments or verticals within their territory. Uses data to refine their plan and consistently builds a pipeline that exceeds targets. Establishes a strong local network.	Is viewed as the go-to-market leader for their region. Develops a sophisticated territory model that becomes a best practice for the team. Uncovers and develops major strategic opportunities that transform the business.

Skill	1. Does not demonstrate competency	2. Partially demonstrates competency	3. Demonstrates competency	4. Sometimes exceeds competency expectations	5. Far exceeds competency expectations
Complex Deal Navigation	Sells to a single contact and struggles to identify key decision-makers. Deals frequently stall due to an inability to manage multiple stakeholders or navigate internal politics.	Can identify multiple stakeholders but has difficulty managing their competing priorities. Relies on a champion but fails to build a broad consensus. Struggles with procurement and legal stages.	Effectively maps the customer's organization and builds relationships with multiple key stakeholders (economic buyer, champion, technical buyer). Manages a clear, stage-based process for complex deals.	Excels at creating and aligning executive-level champions who sell internally on their behalf. Proactively identifies and mitigates deal risks. Skillfully creates urgency and navigates complex procurement and legal reviews.	Is a master deal strategist who can reframe the customer's buying process. Thrives in highly political or competitive situations, building deep executive alliances and creating compelling events that drive deals to a close.

Skill	1. Does not demonstrate competency	2. Partially demonstrates competency	3. Demonstrates competency	4. Sometimes exceeds competency expectations	5. Far exceeds competency expectations
Proactive & Asynchronous Communication	Fails to maintain CRM hygiene, making forecasting impossible. Communication with the London HQ is vague, infrequent, and requires constant follow-up from management.	Updates CRM and communicates with HQ, but inconsistently. Reports tend to lack detail, often requiring clarification calls. Can be slow to respond across time zones.	Maintains a clean, accurate, and up-to-date CRM. Provides clear, concise written updates, enabling asynchronous management. The forecast is reliable. Works effectively with the international team.	Proactively communicates market intelligence, deal risks, and opportunities to the management team. Builds strong cross-functional relationships with the UK team. Is trusted to be the "eyes and ears" in their market.	Is a thought leader in remote communication. Develops processes or templates that the entire team adopts. Serves as an essential bridge between the US field and UK headquarters, effectively translating market needs into action.

Skill	1. Does not demonstrate competency	2. Partially demonstrates competency	3. Demonstrates competency	4. Sometimes exceeds competency expectations	5. Far exceeds competency expectations
Resourcefulness & Autonomy	Needs constant direction and hand-holding. Escalates most problems to their manager without attempting to find a solution. Gives up easily when faced with an obstacle.	Attempts to solve problems but frequently requires validation or assistance. Hesitates to make decisions independently and struggles to manage their time and priorities effectively.	Is a reliable self-starter who requires minimal oversight. Manages their schedule and priorities effectively. When faced with a problem, they research solutions and propose a recommendation.	Proactively identifies and resolves issues before they impact the business. Finds creative solutions to resource constraints. Is highly trusted to operate independently and make sound judgments for the business.	Not only solves their own challenges but also creates new resources, tools, or processes (e.g., a new battlecard, a better ROI calculator) that benefit the entire sales organization, demonstrating a powerful sense of ownership.

Skill	1. Does not demonstrate competency	2. Partially demonstrates competency	3. Demonstrates competency	4. Sometimes exceeds competency expectations	5. Far exceeds competency expectations
Business Acumen	Sells only on features and functions. Is unable to articulate the product's business value or ROI. Is uncomfortable in conversations with senior business leaders.	Can recite standard value propositions but struggles to connect them to a specific customer's unique business context. Has a surface-level understanding of the customer's industry.	Effectively links product capabilities to specific business challenges. Can build a credible business case and communicate the expected ROI to director/VP-level stakeholders.	Confidently leads strategic discussions with C-level executives. Develops customized, sophisticated ROI/TCO models that justify the investment. Is viewed by the customer as a knowledgeable advisor.	Is recognized by customers as a true industry expert. Reshapes the customer's strategic thinking about their own business. Their insights create new, previously unrecognized opportunities for both the customer and the company.

process across multiple candidates, potentially scoring responses with an AI system that interprets the responses.

While these tools can offer a consistent interview to more candidates than any individual could conduct on their own, they also raise ethical questions about what is in the "black box" scoring algorithm.

In 2018, Amazon made headlines for an AI tool they were testing in recruitment that was trained on data submitted by applicants over a 10-year period. Because many of those applicants were men, Reuters reported, the system began penalizing resumes that included the word "women." And while the program was edited to make it neutral on this term, the example highlights the ethical considerations and implications of using potentially biased training data for systems that impact important decisions.

New York City's AI Bias Audit Law requires annual independent and impartial bias audits of automated employment decision tools, and is an example of one of the factors to consider as part of the "Governance and Ethics" pillar of the AI Readiness Maturity Model.

Even if you're confident that the data you're using to train AI tools that assist in the hiring process is free from illegal bias, you'll also want to think cross-functionally about the data being used and what they actually predict. Often, recruiting AI functionality is part of an applicant tracking system managed by HR. If that data is used independently of performance data from the CRM tools managed by RevOps, you run the risk of optimizing your hiring process for the profile of "candidates who get hired," which may not necessarily be the same as "candidates who turn out to be great sellers."

Your AI governance council will want to be sure that you're working cross-functionally on data and technology issues to ensure you're comparing candidates against profiles of prior candidates who turned out to have great business outcomes.

You'll also want to consider a variety of people and cultural issues when implementing these tools as part of a candidate's first exposure to your company. If you're using AI tools as the first screen of your potential human colleagues, don't be surprised when some of the best candidates choose to work for a company that leads with a human connection.

SUCCESSION PLANNING

Aside from sourcing candidates for open positions, the frontline manager (or any manager of people) might also use agents to proactively monitor indicators of succession risks—cohorts of BDRs who are likely to leave in search of the next promotion, territories with senior sellers approaching retirement age, or teams with a number of underperforming sellers—and then conduct additional searches for potential successors to each critical role, based on the required skills and competencies.

HRIS and talent intelligence platforms like **Workday, Cornerstone OnDemand, Eightfold.ai,** and even project management tools like **ClickUp** are increasingly offering AI-driven templates and analytics to identify internal candidates that are ready for their next promotion with the right development plans—or they can manage watchlists of top external candidates in the market to consider for each of these potential succession needs.

By applying AI in this way, talent succession shifts from a reactive fire drill into a proactive, forward-looking, continuous strategic process that anticipates the manager's needs for a sustainable, healthy, productive team.

While promising, you'll also want to ensure that you situate these tools appropriately as aides for managers who want to develop and keep team members, not accelerators to exiting them.

A manager who sees an AI conclusion that a BDR has an "80% chance of leaving the organization" may unconsciously stop investing in their development—thereby causing the departure. If so, an algorithmic bias may have led to the loss of high-potential talent who simply needed a different type of engagement to reduce flight risk—perhaps being rewarded with a spot bonus or included in a special training program for up-and-coming talent to build the competencies they need for the next promotion.

ONBOARDING AND TRAINING

When we've successfully recruited a new seller to the organization, we're excited about their potential—and they're eager to hit the ground running and start closing deals. Yet many organizations offer only a 90-day, "drinking from the firehose" onboarding experience that overwhelms the new hire with more information than they can possibly retain.

As a result, sellers have painfully slow ramp times and a surprisingly high attrition rate, as they fail to gain quick traction in their territories.

AI can transform this process into an efficient, personalized, and data-driven onboarding process that accelerates time to revenue, while building confidence in the manager and the seller in their ability to succeed.

Level 1: Foundational

On-Demand Coach

At the foundational level, the best onboarding programs solve the immediate problem of information overload by delivering information precisely when it's needed—and use AI in this learning environment.

By seeding an LLM with approved case studies and battle cards, a seller can receive a real-time coach they can query at any point in their process. A prompt like "I'm developing a presentation deck for my first

Case Study: Succession Planning with AI-Powered Talent Intelligence

The Challenge

A global automotive supplier faced a dual challenge: a critical shortage of digital talent and a traditionally reactive approach to internal mobility.

As the company pivoted from traditional manufacturing to high-tech automotive software, leadership realized that manual succession planning was a "fire drill" that often overlooked high-potential internal candidates.

The Solution: The Skills-Based Talent Ecosystem

The organization implemented an AI-driven talent intelligence platform to search for candidates inside and outside the organization.

- **Proactive talent rediscovery:** With hundreds of thousands of applications already in their applicant tracking system, the company used AI to refresh profiles with data from public sources and "rediscover" talent for open roles.

- **Predictive promotion readiness:** Rather than waiting for annual reviews, AI continuously monitored an employee's ability to learn skills needed for their next role. In a pilot for a hard-to-staff role, the system mapped the skills of internal candidates to identify who was "ready now" versus "ready in one year," allowing for targeted development interventions.

The ROI

- **Increased internal mobility:** The company achieved greater agility in mobilizing its workforce. As one leader put it: "We have more agility to mobilize and suggest the right job to the right person in the company—and this is a major change."

- **30% recruiter productivity gain:** By automating the initial screening for thousands of applications, recruiters were able

> to focus on the uniquely human skill of candidate relationship building.
>
> - **3.5x conversion on career sites:** The personalized, AI-driven experience significantly increased the rate at which career site visitors converted into applicants.

pitch to this specific customer, who told me in discovery that their biggest pain point is X" can guide sellers to the best stories to tell, ROI calculations to conduct, or demo scripts to present.

Level 2: Advanced

Just in Time Enablement

While an on-demand coach can be a helpful training tool, it's a reactive one that only benefits sellers who are invested in using it. Team-wide platforms like **Seismic, Showpad,** and **Spekit** can proactively be triggered by changes in a CRM record and then surface training videos or other learning materials tagged with the relevant sales stage, industry, product line, and competitor—potentially from right inside the CRM tool itself.

Simulated Role Play

One of the biggest limiters to seller development is the time and availability of qualified managers to conduct practice sessions. Tools like **Quantified.ai, Second Nature,** and **Pitch Monster** address this by creating AI-powered avatars that can engage in simulated sales calls—allowing sellers to role-play with the persona of their choice.

Sellers preparing to deliver a final pitch to a new CFO or a business owner with a limited budget can practice these conversations with the tool, which is designed to respond as those specific personas—and provide feedback on strengths and opportunities for improvement during the call. The seller can continue to repeat these role plays until they are ready to tackle the real thing in their deals.

Role play tools are offered by a variety of vendors, including **Mindtickle, Pitch Monster, Fully Ramped, Hyperbound, Quantified.ai, SecondNature,** and **Allego**.

Level 3: AI-Enabled

By integrating conversational intelligence tools with learning management platforms and simulation tools, an organization might find itself with a truly AI-enabled, personalized, adaptive onboarding program.

In such an environment, the system would analyze the actual sales conversations a seller is having, using conversational intelligence data to identify specific skill gaps for that specific seller—and then auto-enroll them in a certification path for that skill within the learning platform, which requires successful completion of a simulation.

For example, a new seller who is struggling to identify the "paper process" to formalize a purchase after verbal selection might be flagged by the conversational intelligence tool and then assigned a learning path in a platform like **Degreed, Skillsoft,** or **WorkRamp**—which might require a role play with the relevant persona in the sales simulation tool to earn an onboarding completion certificate.

Forecasting

For the frontline sales manager, forecasting has been a mix of art and science, which both have fundamental flaws in their approaches.

On the science side, managers looked at historic win rates for deals, and then applied them to the current pipeline to arrive at a "mathematically calculated forecast" based on a formula like "3% of Stage 1 deal values, 22% of Stage 2," and so on.

That math might work for teams doing a high volume of very similar deals, but it falls apart for teams with lumpier pipelines. While it might be true that over the last 12 months the team closed 60% of the revenue that made it to Stage 3, this insight isn't helpful in a quarter with only one Stage 3 deal in the pipeline. If it's a million-dollar deal, the team is either going to win it or not—the closed revenue will either be $1M or zero—and a $600k forecast is going to miss the mark widely in either scenario.

To mitigate this challenge, frontline managers often adopt a "commitment" process—using a more artful, personal experience-led determination about whether a deal should be in or out of the forecast for this period.

The weekly forecasting meeting then becomes a painful ritual, in which managers interrogate sellers whose reports on their deals are unreliable at best. Some sellers provide overconfident estimates due to "happy ears" or a fear of delivering disappointing news, while others sandbag so they can later be seen as heroes who overperform against a lowball number.

The manager manually rolls these numbers into a spreadsheet and presents them to their manager with some gut-level adjustments, producing a number that senior leadership doesn't trust and feels they need to interrogate themselves, kicking off the next cycle of scrutiny.

Level 1: Foundational

At the most basic level, a frontline manager can improve their ability to deliver a commitment-driven forecast number by using an LLM like **Gemini** or **ChatGPT** to act as an objective, data-driven "third voice" in the conversations they have with their sellers.

With a bit of background information, such tools can help interrogate the details of an opportunity to clarify the issues at stake in determining whether the deal is in, out, or a stretch opportunity.

A prompt like "I'm leading a sales team that uses the MEDDPICC framework to evaluate opportunities and would like your assistance in thinking through whether to put this deal in the forecast" is a great starting point for a brief interaction where details about the opportunity, contacts, and activities conducted so far can be shared—and the ultimate decision of "to include it or not" is more likely to come from a consistent set of criteria across each deal.

By using these tools in real time with their sellers, a frontline manager can also model the behavior—increasing their team members' ability to conduct ad hoc assessments at any time of the week—not just during a weekly forecast meeting.

Level 2: Advanced

When teams adopt AI tools more broadly, though, they can begin creating highly reliable forecasts—good or bad—and shift their attention to activities that influence the deals inside it.

Calling the Number

Revenue intelligence and predictive forecasting platforms—like **Clari**, **Insight Squared**, and **Forecastio**—can create art- and science-based forecasts with a much more granular level of inspection—at a much wider scale—than ever before.

By broadening their focus beyond a deal's *stage* to a range of other data points, AI tools can calculate a unique probability of closure for each deal in the pipeline. They can also eliminate seller bias by looking beyond the static CRM fields sellers manually update, drawing additional context from the entire sales ecosystem. By bringing in email data, conversational intelligence, and calendar events to analyze what's actually happening in a deal—not just the seller's opinion—AI tools produce a multidimensional picture of each deal's true health and momentum.

For each deal, the AI tool can look through thousands of previous deals—won and lost—to identify those with the most similar patterns. This insight can be built by combining structured descriptive data (such as deal size, opportunity age, seller name, and the number of times a close date has been pushed out) with engagement data (like email response rates, meeting attendance patterns, the number of stakeholders involved from the prospect, and whether those contacts include senior decision-makers). Conversational intelligence data can delve into the transcripts of those calls and meetings to detect mentions of competitors, conversations about budget and pricing, and the objections raised by key decision-makers to provide additional context on the deal.

From this vantage point, the AI tool asks "When we've seen deals with this specific combination of size, industry, engagement, and competition before, what was the outcome?"—and those answers can then be aggregated to provide a total forecast range and probability score like "There is an 85% probability of landing between $1.9M and $2.1M."

In my own application of Clari's AI for this purpose, I was able to successfully call the final quarter's forecast with 95% accuracy by the second week of the quarter, for 16 out of 17 quarters straight (business disruptions caused by COVID shutdowns in the final three weeks of one quarter creating the anomaly in March of 2020).

Within a few months of using AI tools to call the number successfully, the frontline manager will find that their conversations with their VP are no longer tied up with long interrogations of "Are you sure this is the number?" Instead, the leadership team understands that it's highly likely to land as predicted and turns their conversation to what to do about it.

Similarly, when a frontline manager includes these insights into forecast discussions with their team members, they can shift their focus from simply asking "Are you sure about this deal?" to a more productive "Our AI tool is giving this deal a 30% win probability because we haven't engaged with a senior decision-maker in six weeks—where their last conversation included some detailed questions about how we compared to a competitor. What's our plan to address that?"

The manager needs to be careful, however, not to rely on the AI tool to inform performance or employment decisions. While it may be fine to use a low-likelihood-of-winning score as a jumping-off point to work with a seller on improving their deal strategy, the conversation should never progress to one like "The AI forecasts that you will miss quota, so I'm starting an exit plan for you." While it is possible that the AI tool's prediction of missed quota is correct, the "black box" nature of their predictions is a legally untenable basis for termination—a place where a living, breathing person (and all of their uniquely human abilities) is best positioned to make decisions.

Influencing the Number

When managers adopt AI tools to create accurate forecasts, they can also shift their attention from defending the number to influencing the deals within it. The same analysis used to create the forecast call can help the AI tool flag risk criteria for sellers, who can then act on the insights to course-correct. A manager may look at these signals and coach their sellers with insightful questions, like:

- **Stage velocity**: Typical deals we win are in stage 2 for an average of 17 days. Your deal has been there for 35. Perhaps it is not important to the prospect anymore?

- **Engagement gaps**: This prospect typically responds to emails within 48 hours. Your last three messages for the previous two weeks have gone unanswered. Perhaps your contact has left the organization?

- **Stakeholder coverage**: This deal does not engage the individual named as the economic buyer. Perhaps you're not multi-threaded enough in this deal?

By allowing AI tools to surface statistical anomalies, the manager no longer has to go hunting for problems; they can spend their time in deal reviews focusing on what matters most: coaching their sellers on the specific actions they can take to mitigate potential risks in their deals.

Level 3: AI-Enabled

Modeling Multiple Outcomes

Because AI tools have access to these forecasting signals in every deal, advanced organizations might shift from a weekly forecasting cadence to a system of continuous forecasting and outcome modeling.

Leaders who know that they have an 85% chance of landing in a specific forecast range could start using AI to answer questions like:

- Show me the most efficient path to our "best case" number. Which specific deals do we need to accelerate, and which executives are the best ones to introduce into the conversations?

- I'm considering offering a one-time pricing discount to help close some of my marginal deals this quarter. Based on prior patterns, which of my current opportunities would be likely to accelerate their decision in exchange for a discount of what size—and what would the projected forecast be as a result?

Vendors like **Clari** and **Revcast** have already built scenario modeling tools that advance capabilities in this direction, while investors in companies like **Dealcode.ai** and **Relevance AI** envision the ability to create AI agents that proactively generate offerings and A/B test their impact on live deals in the pipeline.

Managers will want to remember that their human intuition also has a role to play—an AI tool that suggests a discount to close a deal this quarter may not have the same ability to detect "bluffing" that the human in the room does, and may miss that the buyer was actually prepared to pay full price or more on the same timeline.

Case Study: Revenue Growth Through AI-Powered Pricing

A leading international mobility provider, operating in over 140 countries and generating nearly €3B in annual revenue, successfully transitioned from a fragmented legacy pricing system to a unified AI-driven platform—redefining the organization's approach to dynamic pricing and capacity management.

The Challenge: Fragmented Systems and Manual Constraints

The organization previously relied on a pricing infrastructure made up of three large, disconnected tools. It created several bottlenecks:

- **Operational inefficiency:** Pricing analysts were forced to perform manual data entry across multiple systems, leaving little time for strategic analysis.

- **Lack of agility:** The systems could only handle a limited number of daily rate changes, with long loading times preventing the company from capturing real-time market opportunities.

- **Limited visibility:** Forecasting capabilities were short-term and lacked granularity. Pricing actions did not feed back into demand forecasts, creating a disconnect between strategy and execution.

- **Static offerings:** The company struggled to deploy flexible mobility services or bundled corporate packages due to technological limitations.

The Solution: AI-Powered Pricing and Revenue Management

The company chose a global AI-powered pricing platform to serve as the cornerstone of its digital transformation. By integrating price optimization, revenue management, and configure-price-quote (CPQ) capabilities into a single source of truth, the organization achieved:

- **Automated agility:** Transitioned from manual updates to automated, hourly price triggers across car categories, locations, and rental durations.

> - **Granular demand forecasting:** Developed the ability to plan activity weeks and months in advance based on sophisticated KPIs like revenue, rental volume, and total rental days.
> - **Optimized capacity control:** Gained the insight to steer fleet distribution toward the most profitable customer segments and tailor offers to specific traveler needs.
> - **Talent Evolution:** Applied a new organizational approach to the project, with a focus on shifting the "pricing analyst" role into a more strategic "demand analyst" role.
>
> **The ROI**
>
> The solution significantly beat the company's expectations:
>
> - **Revenue growth:** Achieved 7.1% year-over-year revenue growth, when the original target was 1.7%.
> - **Employee adoption:** 89% of employees reported that the new smart pricing tools helped them generate more business.

SALES & MARKETING COLLABORATION ON LEAD MANAGEMENT

As the internet has made more information about vendors available to prospects with more simplicity than ever before, analysts have noted that buyers are now anonymously getting much further down the buying journey before they've even filled out a form or spoken with a seller.

These buyers are often called the "dark funnel," and AI tools can use intent data to shine light on them earlier.

Level 1: Foundational

At the foundational level, simple if/then rules can be put in place to automate the earliest steps of engagement with an identified lead. "IF a prospect in my territory has filled out a form requesting a demo, THEN send an automated message with my calendar availability, and notify my BDR to follow up within 60 minutes" is an example of the workflow automation that **HubSpot** and **Outreach** have made standard for identified leads in many selling organizations.

Level 2: Advanced

We begin moving into more advanced use cases when we start thinking about how to use intent data to trigger these engagements with non-identified, anonymous prospects.

Intent data can come both from your own organization, identifying what buyers are doing on the digital properties you own (like your website, blog, and social media pages), and those you don't—including a network of B2B publisher websites, blogs, and forums.

A starting point is to use intent data providers such as **6sense, ZoomInfo,** or **Demandbase** to conduct reverse IP lookups and match the IP addresses of anonymous visitors to specific companies.

AI features (like **HubSpot**'s Buyer Intent, powered by **Clearbit**) extend this story by tracking which pages they view on your site, long page dwell times, and other behavioral data to create an "intent score"—and dedicated tools like **Lift.ai** take the idea a step further to use a pretrained machine learning model to score the real-time behavior of every visitor (anonymous or not), predict their likelihood to convert, and trigger a live chat prompt on your integrated tool for only the visitors who are showing a very high level of intent.

Tools like **Bombora** and **G2** act as third-party intent data aggregators to monitor content consumption across thousands of B2B websites, identifying prospects who are researching you or your competitors on sites that aren't your own.

When we shift the conversation from identifying "Who has high intent today?" to "Who will have intent tomorrow?", we're moving into a more sophisticated use case for AI in the lead management area. When we integrate our own CRM data with data from intent providers, we can also start using AI to understand account-wide signals and prioritize our sales and marketing efforts accordingly.

Level 3: AI-Enabled

A high-intent prospect is only valuable to an organization, though, if it's given to a seller capable of bringing them through the buyer journey.

Traditional lead distribution is often simplistic, relying on a basic round-robin or territory assignment. This is inefficient and fails to match opportunity with skill.

AI-powered lead scoring and qualification systems create the possibility of doing something far more sophisticated. Using machine learning, these tools analyze hundreds of signals in real time—including firmographic data (company size, industry), demographic data (job title), website behavior (pages visited, content downloaded), and third-party intent data (what topics the company is researching online).

Based on this holistic view, the AI predicts each lead's conversion likelihood with high precision, automatically prioritizing the highest-quality prospects.

For the frontline manager, some AI vendors suggest the game-changing possibility of orchestrating the *distribution* of these scored leads to the seller most likely to close them.

Instead of a one-size-fits-all approach, the fully integrated system can implement sophisticated routing rules like:

- A high-value lead from a Fortune 500 company showing strong buying intent can be routed directly to a senior account executive with a proven track record in enterprise sales.

- A smaller, more transactional lead from a mid-market company can be assigned to a junior seller who is building their skills.

- A lead with technical questions can be routed to a seller with a stronger product background.

This intelligent orchestration ensures that the best opportunities are always handled by the best-suited sellers, maximizing the conversion probability of every lead and optimizing the entire team's efficiency.

However, this area, too, is one where ethics, fairness, and legal compliance are critical risk issues to monitor.

When I was a quota-carrying seller, I was frustrated by a manager who modified sales territories so that some of the "best" and largest leads were given to a seller with whom he had a close personal relationship. When that seller successfully closed these accounts for larger-than-average contract sizes, the manager used it as proof of the seller's superiority—and used that data as a pretext to carve out an even larger territory for the seller. Eventually, enough sellers got frustrated enough to ask HR to intervene—and when an independent analyst redrew our territories, the entire team's performance improved.

When we use AI for lead scoring and routing, we risk creating a self-reinforcing understanding of data—and systemically disenfranchising sellers from equal opportunity to achieve their quotas. If you route opportunities to sellers based on a belief that one seller is more likely to close it than another, you might also want to automatically assign the less-qualified seller to shadow the higher-performing one so they gain the skills necessary to be given more opportunities like it in the future.

Given the potential for introducing systemic bias and unfair working conditions, you'll also want to take a deep look at data cleanliness and readiness before deploying AI for these kinds of use cases—and then you should only proceed with strong legal and ethical guidance from your governance council.

SALES AND MARKETING PROCESS ENFORCEMENT

One of the greatest sources of friction between managers and their teams is the perception of micromanagement, particularly around

CRM hygiene and process adherence—and AI tools can provide a solution that allows for accountability without constant oversight.

Level 1: Foundational

AI-powered sales engagement platforms provide managers with clear, at-a-glance dashboards that monitor process adherence automatically. A manager can instantly see if sellers are following the prescribed sales stages *and* completing follow-up tasks on time through a dashboard in **Salesforce** or other CRM tools—while cadences built into **Outreach** or **Salesloft** can ensure sellers are automatically using the approved messaging from the living playbook in various tasks.

By incorporating these out-of-the-box features into daily work, managers don't need to manually inspect every contact record or constantly chase team members for updates. This allows them to manage by exception, focusing their valuable one-on-one time on strategic coaching and deal support, rather than acting as the "CRM police."

This shift elevates the manager from a reactive process enforcer to a proactive process architect. In the traditional model, a manager spends an inordinate amount of time asking, "Did you update the CRM?" or "Did you follow the steps?"—but when AI is used to automate the guidance and enforcement of these issues, the manager's job becomes far more strategic.

The central question is no longer "Did you follow the process?" but rather "Is the process we've designed the most effective one?" The manager can leverage AI's analysis as a feedback loop to A/B test different playbook messages, experiment with different lead routing rules, or identify bottlenecks in the sales cycle.

As a result, they are no longer just managing their sellers; they are managing the processes their sellers use to produce the results—elevating their role to that of a systems thinker who is constantly designing, testing, and optimizing the sales engine to drive predictable growth.

Within the prescribed process, there is also an opportunity to help every seller or marketer make their communications better, faster, and more effective. Tools like **Lavender** and **Regie.ai** integrate directly into a user's existing email client and act as real-time writing partners—providing suggestions to improve clarity, tone, and the likelihood of getting a reply in real time based on millions of data points.

Professionals who know the next step in their sales process can offer up a writing prompt, such as "Send a follow-up email to this decision-maker who didn't make it to our demo meeting," and receive a drafted message to refine a few seconds later.

Level 2: Advanced

As individual message quality is enhanced, the next level of evolution is to use AI to ensure that a prospect receives a high-quality, cohesive, personalized series of communications across multiple channels over time.

Sales engagement platforms like **Outreach** and **Salesloft** have long been leaders in this space, and can now use AI to analyze historical performance data to suggest the optimal number of steps in a communications sequence, the best time of day to send the message, and the best wording of the message based on robust A/B testing to continually improve performance.

By leveraging generative AI within the platform, features like **Outreach**'s "Smart Email Assist" can also create replies to customer communications that are contextually relevant, based on its analysis of prior conversation history—ensuring a seamless conversation across time.

Level 3: AI-Enabled

For the fully integrated organization, AI agents may take over much of the early stages of a conversation with prospects—researching each prospect company using its integrated data sources. By leveraging generative AI, these agents might craft and execute a multichannel outreach sequence, managing basic follow-ups and email responses—and then seamlessly hand them off to a human account executive when a prospect shows both significant engagement and positive intent.

As one step toward this fully integrated vision, vendors like **Drop Cowboy** and **Voicedrop.ai** offer "ringless voicemail" solutions which deliver prerecorded voice messages directly to a recipient's inbox without causing their phone to ring—and their advances in voice cloning offer the promise of conducting A/B tests to determine which messages (or voices) gain the best callback rates.

As described elsewhere, you'll want to weigh issues of authenticity, trust, and customer experience in these automated interactions— thinking about how transparently you want to make the handoff from AI persona to live seller, and whether your application complies with the evolving legal landscape surrounding the synthetic creation of a real person's voice, image, and likeness.

IN SUM

For the frontline sales manager, the true promise of AI is the ability to fundamentally reclaim time and, therefore, change what they do in their role. Under constant pressure to produce revenue, time-crunched leaders often believe the fastest route is to revert to "super-seller" mode—stepping in to close deals themselves at the first sign their team member is struggling.

The AI-supported leader, however, breaks this career-stalling bottleneck by systematically offloading the exhaustive administrative inspection required for forecasting, QBR preparation, deal reviews, and talent documentation to tools that can take on these jobs.

By automating the data collection and synthesis components of these tasks, AI allows the manager to pivot from being an inspector of the past to an architect of future performance. AI also expands the manager's reach, coaching sellers and reinforcing best practices even on calls the manager isn't part of.

For those discussions the manager can participate in, AI tools also synthesize vast amounts of data to help them prioritize the most critical, high-leverage questions to ask—shifting the focus from unreliable gut-feel to data-driven strategic coaching.

This transformation elevates the manager from a reactive process *enforcer* to a proactive systems *thinker* who architects better future performance, ensuring that their invaluable human experience is applied only to the most strategic activities, where it can maximize team revenue and long-term talent development.

Here is a table that summarizes the key processes, tasks, and AI applications discussed in this chapter:

Process Stage	Specific Task	AI Application	Example Vendors/Products
Coaching	Measuring basic communication skills and identifying coaching themes	Conversational Intelligence Analysis (talk-to-listen ratios, sentiment, topic tracking)	Gong, Chrous.ai, Avoma, Dialpad
	Spotlighting team-wide trends for group development	Playbook-based trend analysis across all calls	Gong, Chorus.ai, Avoma, Dialpad
	Providing objective, automated scoring for every call	Automated call scoring against a predefined scorecard	Gong, Chorus.ai, Avoma, Dialpad
	Diagnosing individual skill gaps and assigning tailored training	Prescriptive coaching & automated learning path assignment	Integrated learning/ simulation platforms
Deal Reviews	Eliminating drudgery by pre-analyzing call data	AI-generated meeting summaries, transcripts, and opportunity analysis reports	Zoom, Microsoft Teams, Fireflies.ai, Otter.ai, Gemini, ChatGPT
	Providing data-driven health scores and flagging risks	Deal health scoring & risk factor identification	Clari, Outreach, Salesloft

Process Stage	Specific Task	AI Application	Example Vendors/Products
	Proactively scheduling reviews and providing prescriptive recommendations	Proactive signal detection & prescriptive next-step recommendations	Clari, Outreach, Salesloft
Territory Management & QBRs	Automating the creation of QBR presentation drafts	Generative AI for deck creation from CRM reports and templates	AppEQ, Matik.io, Rollstack, Gemini (in Slides), Beautiful.ai, Canva
	Informing territory plans with predictive insights	Deal-level risk analysis, predictive lead scoring, narrative account prioritization	Clari, Outreach, HubSpot Sales Hub, Pocus
	Designing territory strategy through data-driven simulations	Scenario modeling & probabilistic outcome assessment	Advanced AI agents

Process Stage	Specific Task	AI Application	Example Vendors/Products
Talent Management	Automating notetaking for 1:1s	Automated meeting transcription & summarization	Zoom AI Companion, Fathom, Otter.ai, Microsoft Teams
	Proactively suggesting 1:1 agenda items	Proactive agenda suggestion based on CRM and meeting history	Fellow, ClickUp
	Creating pre-meeting intelligence briefings	Synthesis of call recordings and CRM data for pre-meeting briefings	Integrated AI agents
	Drafting performance reviews	Generative AI for drafting review narratives	Gemini, ChatGPT, Claude
	Compiling and analyzing performance data to counter biases	Data synthesis from CRM, conversational intelligence, and 360-degree feedback	Gong, Clari, Salesforce, Betterworks, Lattice, PerformYard
	Crafting compelling and precise job descriptions	Generative AI for job description drafting & optimization	Claude, ChatGPT, Gemini, Grammarly Business, Workable, Textio, Datapeople
	Proactively sourcing passive candidates	AI agent-based candidate sourcing & talent rediscovery	Eightfold.ai, Beamery, SeekOut

Process Stage	Specific Task	AI Application	Example Vendors/Products
	Crafting interview questions and scoring rubrics	Generative AI for creating structured interview kits	Claude, ChatGPT, Gemini
	Screening resumes with natural language understanding	AI-powered resume parsing and skill inference	Eightfold.ai, Beamery, SeekOut
	Conducting and scoring one-way video interviews	AI-scored asynchronous video interviews	HireVue, Phenom
	Providing an on-demand coach for new hires	Queryable LLMs seeded with company-specific content	Gemini, ChatGPT
	Surfacing "just-in-time" learning content	Proactive content surfacing triggered by CRM events	Seismic, Showpad, Spekit
	Providing a safe environment for simulated role-play	AI-powered avatars for simulated sales calls	Quantified.ai, Second Nature, Pitch Monster, Mindtickle, Fully Ramped, Hyperbound, Allego

Process Stage	Specific Task	AI Application	Example Vendors/Products
	Creating personalized, adaptive onboarding programs	Integrated skill gap analysis & automated certification path enrollment	Degreed, Skillsoft, WorkRamp
Forecasting	Acting as an objective third voice in 1:1 forecast discussions	LLM-based deal interrogation against a sales framework	Gemini, ChatGPT
	"Calling the number" with high accuracy	Predictive forecasting based on multi-factor deal-level analysis	Clari, InsightSquared, Forecastio
	"Influencing the number" by flagging specific risks for coaching	Surfacing statistical anomalies (e.g., stage velocity, engagement gaps)	Clari, InsightSquared, Forecastio
	Modeling multiple outcomes and running "what-if" scenarios	Scenario modeling for best-case paths or impact of discounts	Clari, Revcast, Dealcode.ai, Relevance AI
Lead Management	Automating initial engagement with identified leads	Simple if-then workflow automation	HubSpot, Outreach

Process Stage	Specific Task	AI Application	Example Vendors/Products
	Identifying anonymous prospects and scoring their intent	Reverse IP lookups, behavioral intent scoring, third-party intent data aggregation	6sense, ZoomInfo, Demandbase, HubSpot (powered by Clearbit), Lift.ai, Bombora, G2
Process Enforcement	Monitoring process adherence automatically	Automated dashboards for sales stage adherence and task completion	Salesforce, Outreach, Salesloft
	Optimizing multi-channel communication sequences	AI-driven suggestions for sequence steps, timing, and wording	Outreach, Salesloft
	Automating early-stage prospect conversations	AI Agents for automated research, outreach, and initial response handling	Outreach, Salesloft, Drop Cowboy, Voicedrop.ai
	Writing assistance	Help sellers make communications within the process more effective	Lavender, Regie.ai

AI FOR THE STRATEGY SETTING CRO

When you're a sales leader, your work becomes a lot less about day-to-day operations and a lot more about cross-company collaboration and strategy setting. Because the CRO tends to implement processes and technologies across the GTM organization—and potentially other departments in the company—their AI applications tend to fall within Level 2: Advanced or Level 3: AI-Enabled frameworks. However, there are still a few opportunities for them to employ foundational-level tactics, too.

TAM ANALYSIS FOR NEW LOGO MOTIONS

For many CROs, the strategic revenue plan begins with two simple questions: "Who are all of the prospects that might buy our product," and "How much are their potential contracts worth?"

The answers to these questions inform everything from the amount an investor will invest in the business and the sizing and scaling of the sales and marketing teams' budgets to the crafting of individual-level territories and sales targets.

Historically, these questions get answered with either a top-down approach (that begins with broad industry research from firms like Gartner or Forrester, and uses SIC and NAICS codes to narrow down relevant segments of the market), or a bottom-up method that attempts to explicitly name each potential account that fits the ideal customer profile.

While each approach has its benefits, both are limited by being single-point-in-time snapshots of the market. Building them is a labor-intensive process, often relying on data that is months or even years out of date—and they do nothing to answer the question "Where should a sales team spend its time *this week* to have the biggest impact?"

Traditionally, conversations about the total addressable market (TAM) are actually talking about a few nested concepts. At the broadest level, the TAM defines the universe in which a company operates. Within the TAM, the service addressable market (SAM) defines the portion they can reasonably serve given their unique geographic and product/market fit constraints, and the service obtainable market (SOM) is an even smaller subset that defines the portion they can capture given available resources and competitive dynamics.

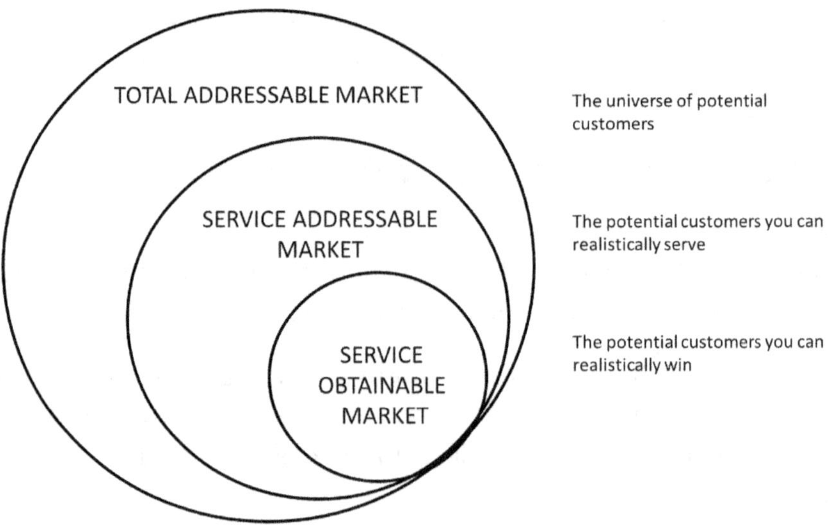

Figure 1: The Nested TAM, SAM, and SOM Models

AI tools can transform this understanding of the market from a static, backward-looking description of all possible accounts to a dynamic, forward-looking map that shows where potential buying activity is concentrating.

Level 1: Foundational

At the foundational level, generative AI tools such as **ChatGPT, Gemini,** or **Claude** can speed the process of collecting and synthesizing data to define the various markets. Instead of wading through disparate systems, a revenue operations professional could feed these tools multiple reports and prompt them to describe TAM, SAM, and SOM with a prompt like "Please review the attached market reports from Gartner, Forrester, and IDC. Create an estimate of the number of accounts and size of opportunity I can realistically address with my service, which is available in the US, Canada, and the United Kingdom, and has the core capabilities described in the attached feature list."

Level 2: Advanced

Packaged data providers like **ZoomInfo, Cognism,** and **Apollo.io** can assist in creating a bottom-up census of accounts in each category, aggregating, deduplicating, and enriching data on millions of global companies to assist the sales leader with creating targetable lists for their teams.

Augmenting this analysis with intent data from vendors like **6sense** or **Demandbase** has helped many sales leaders to prioritize weekly activity informed by the digital body language that SAM or SOM prospects are displaying.

Level 3: AI-Enabled

Perhaps the most exciting potential for AI in this area lies in augmenting external data with information produced in-house—through analysis of call recordings, emails, and CRM data—and allowing an AI agent to identify customer segments that might not otherwise be immediately obvious.

Rather than simply searching for all of the retailers in the United States that had more than a certain number of new store openings last year, an AI agent might identify a previously unknown segment of "value-driven buyers" who frequently ask about a specific ROI metric in sales calls and who convert to paying customers more frequently than those who don't.

Moreover, the agent might be deployed on a 24/7 market analysis project to continuously monitor a set of real-time data sources—news feeds, regulatory filings, social media channels, industry websites, and third-party intent providers—to continuously update the SAM and SOM lists (and, as a result, the list of targets for marketers and sellers to focus on) in real time.

Creating these tools would require a robust MLOps infrastructure, with integration into internal systems such as **Gong**'s Data Cloud, CRM tools, email systems, and a wide variety of external data feeds.

As organizations move toward AI-driven market intelligence, the CRO must prioritize the quality and diversity of their data sources. Because AI analysis is only as good as the data it ingests, tools that over-index on easy-to-scrape sources—such as tech or healthcare firms with massive digital footprints—often overlook industries with lower digital maturity, like law firms or manufacturing.

Sales teams that focus exclusively on these over-digitized hunting grounds risk competing in a crowded market against every other company that uses the same biased data. To maintain a competitive advantage, the CRO must ensure its AI models are identifying the "dark TAM"—profitable, less-digitized sectors that competitors have overlooked.

Continually asking "Where has our data come from?" and comparing its output to what feels sensible based on industry knowledge will help you to avoid competing exclusively in red oceans unnecessarily.

PARTNER REVENUE-GENERATING STRATEGIES

PARTNER IDENTIFICATION AND RECRUITMENT

The company's revenue doesn't just come from direct sales motions, though. Many CROs plan to retire part of their growth targets through a network of partners and resellers who sell on their behalf.

Yet in many organizations, the development of this network has been opportunistic or reactive. A great conversation at a tradeshow or a haphazard introduction through an existing customer can lead to signing an agreement with a partner who may or may not be effective. Many cycles are wasted on training and onboarding the partner, and significant revenue may not come for years—if at all.

AI has the possibility of applying more scientific discipline to the partner recruitment process by defining exactly what "good" looks like and then systematically finding partners who match that profile at scale.

Level 1: Foundational

It starts with creating a clear definition of what a great partner is—and generative AI can help refine your thinking in this process.

You might use a tool like **ChatGPT, Gemini,** or **Claude** as a brainstorming partner, beginning with a prompt like "I am the head of partnerships for an enterprise software company selling revenue management systems to hotels. Help me build an ideal partner profile (IPP) for a new reseller we want to recruit in the Asia/Pacific region. Key competencies we value include existing relationships with owner/operators of franchised hotels, a technical staff familiar with multi-tenant cloud deployments, and experience selling complementary solutions like property management systems or bookings platforms."

Through a conversational process, AI can help flesh out a detailed, multifaceted profile that goes beyond basic demographics to identify a list of potential partners to approach.

You can then prompt the tool to generate a series of personalized outreach email templates—each tailored to the specific value proposition for that potential partner in their local language. This simple exercise elevates your initial outreach from generic form letters to compelling, relevant invitations that demonstrate you've done your homework.

Level 2: Advanced

Specialized partner ecosystem platforms now use AI to add more value to this exercise by incorporating insight from a wide variety of public and proprietary datasets. These tools may help identify potential partners based on an understanding of their stated technology focus, the tech stack they use internally, the industries they serve, their key customers, and even signals that suggest a cultural fit. This is "smart partner matching," and it dramatically accelerates the top of your recruitment funnel.

PartnerOptimizer is one such example—analyzing your current partners, helping you build a data-driven IPP based on your top performers, and then generating a list of new recruitment targets that are "lookalikes" of your best partners. Similarly, platforms like **Mindmatrix** BridgeAI explore both structured and unstructured data to help you recruit the best partners with greater precision.

Level 3: AI-Enabled

At the highest level of sophistication, AI agents don't just identify potential partners; they autonomously manage the entire top-of-funnel recruitment process.

In this model, an AI agent is configured with the data-driven attributes of your top-performing partners. It then continuously scans the market—monitoring news, press releases, technology directories, and professional networks—to identify new companies that fit this lookalike model.

When a high-potential partner is identified, the agent can score their fit, generate a hyper-personalized outreach message referencing a specific, relevant trigger event (such as a recent product launch or customer win), and even manage the initial back-and-forth email conversation.

The AI handles prospecting, qualification, and initial engagement, and hands off the lead to a human partner account manager once the potential partner has expressed genuine interest.

While this end-to-end automation is still emerging in the PRM space, the technological blueprint is well established in HR tech for employee recruitment and should represent the next generation of partner-management capabilities.

As with the use of autonomous agents described previously, these use cases require careful planning by your governance council to protect your brand reputation, with particular attention given to authenticity and transparency. Deciding when and how to disclose a bot's role in partner engagement and determining the boundary between targeted personalization and digital stalking are critical issues to tackle. Ultimately, a business partnership is one between groups of human beings who operate with deep interpersonal trust and collaboration—the use of AI for partner recruitment should facilitate, not fake, that work.

PARTNER ENABLEMENT

Once you've successfully recruited a promising partner, you need to enable them. Many of the same challenges that exist for enabling your own sellers exist for the channel, too—with the added complexity that they don't work for your company and are even one more step removed from your day-to-day supervision and control.

Many partner onboarding programs hope for the best by giving new partners an avalanche of documents, training modules, and administrative tasks to complete to earn an "official certification." It can result in a very slow ramp time and—in many cases—a disengaged partner who quietly churns before they ever close a deal.

AI offers a path to transform this process by moving from a generic information dump to a personalized, automated journey that accelerates each partner's unique path to their first dollar of revenue.

Case Study: Scaling Revenue Productivity in a Global Partner Ecosystem

The Challenge

A network infrastructure provider relied on a complex, global mix of direct sellers and thousands of channel partners, whose mindshare they had to compete for against other products they're selling, to sell a complex portfolio of solutions that require mastery of lots of different information.

The Solution: The Unified Sales Readiness Framework

The organization transitioned from a fragmented collection of portals to a centralized AI-powered sales-readiness platform designed to serve the needs of direct and indirect sellers.

- **Single source of truth for content:** The company consolidated all sales assets into a single, searchable repository, using AI to tag and recommend content based on seller roles and buyer personas.

- **Correlating readiness to revenue:** The solution hyper-personalizes at scale, allowing the company's development approach to move beyond "completion tracking," shifting the mindset from "training" to "enablement."

The ROI

- **70% of target users** adopted the system for personal training, compared to 15% who historically attended training webinars.

- Leadership attributes the improvement in training to more than **40% growth in sales achievement** year over year.

Level 1: Foundational

The first step in maturing your onboarding process is to eliminate the manual, repetitive tasks that consume your team's time and create friction for the partner. This is less about deep intelligence and more about applying basic process automation to a standard checklist of activities.

Nearly every modern PRM platform includes workflow automation capabilities that can serve as the engine for a foundational onboarding program. When a new partner has been signed, the system can automatically trigger a predefined sequence of events. It might send a welcome email with portal login credentials, deliver the standard product overview deck, prompt the partner to complete legal and financial paperwork, and schedule a 30-day check-in with the assigned partner account manager.

Solutions like **Impartner's** Journey Builder and **ZINFI**'s Partner Onboarding Manager enable you to create automated, step-by-step onboarding paths, ensuring a consistent, repeatable experience for every new partner. Similarly, **PartnerStack** helps you guide new partners through the early stages of onboarding by creating automated email sequences.

Even tools focused on document processing, such as **Datamatics** Copilot, can play a role here by using AI to ensure partners submit the required documents for compliance in the countries and regions they operate in.

Level 2: Advanced

The next level of sophistication moves beyond automating a standard onboarding process for all partners to one that is personalized for each partner's unique business context.

Here, the AI tool analyzes a new partner's attributes—their partner type (reseller, ISV, or consultant), tier level, geographic region, or even their stated business goals—and then dynamically assembles a relevant onboarding curriculum.

Instead of a single, one-size-fits-all training program, the partner is presented with a set of modules, content, and tasks that are directly applicable to their role in your ecosystem. For example, a simple referral partner might be guided through product definitions and lead registration processes to get started, while a systems integrator may first be offered API documentation and technical sandboxes to work in.

PRM vendors are increasingly building this intelligence into their platforms. For example, **Journeybee** offers a configurable journey builder that allows you to design unique onboarding paths for each partner segment. You can define the stages and activities, and the platform automatically guides the partner through their specific onboarding path.

Mindmatrix offers "dynamic persona-driven onboarding workflows" to achieve a similar result, and **ZINFI** leverages AI to analyze partner data and personalize the entire partner journey, including the delivery of tailored training content and marketing materials.

Level 3: AI-Enabled

At the fully AI-enabled level, partner onboarding is an adaptive, real-time learning journey. This moves beyond predefined paths for different personas and creates a truly one-to-one onboarding experience for every single partner, scaled across your entire ecosystem.

In this model, an AI agent might act as a personal tutor for each new partner—continuously monitoring their real-time engagement and performance during the onboarding process. It might track which training modules they complete, how they score on certification quizzes, what content they download from the portal, and where they spend the most time. Then, based on this continuous stream of data, the AI would dynamically adjust the partner's onboarding path on the fly.

For instance, if a partner's employee repeatedly fails a quiz on competitive positioning, the AI might automatically assign a remedial micro-learning video on that topic and suggest a role-play simulation to practice objection handling. Conversely, if a partner's technical team breezes through the initial API training, the AI might unlock advanced integration modules ahead of schedule.

This creates a hyper-efficient and maximally effective learning environment, ensuring each partner gets exactly the support they need, precisely when they need it. And while the capability is still emerging, it's the clear direction the market is heading in.

Platforms like **Disco.co** describe these as "AI-generated learning flows" that create customized educational pathways that adapt in real time. Platforms like **Allego** emphasize "customized sales training with AI-powered learning, personalized coaching, and just-in-time resources" for skills enablement.

When deploying AI tools for partner onboarding and training, your governance council will want to pay attention to which proprietary or confidential information is feeding the models (and ultimately making its way out of your organization to your partner) and ensure appropriate data governance rules, retention policies, and confidentiality agreements are in place.

ENABLING PARTNERS WHEN THEY NEED IT

One of the biggest challenges I've encountered with partner programs is keeping the attention of the specific employees at that partner who I expect to deliver revenue. We may have spent a long time with the senior leaders of an organization, getting them excited about the possibility of the partnership, but deals are won or lost at the field level. If the frontline sellers on the partner's team don't have the same enthusiasm as their leaders—or are distracted by a big portfolio of solutions from other vendors that they can sell just as easily—we're not going to see the result we want.

AI offers the potential to stay top-of-mind with these sellers by delivering the right content, training, and guidance to your partners right when they need it, empowering them to sell with the same confidence and competence as your internal team.

Level 1: Foundational

The most basic challenge here is in helping partners find the information they need to do their jobs. A partner seller who can't quickly find a pricing sheet or the latest competitive battle card is likely to give up and sell something easier. The foundational level of AI addresses this challenge by embedding intelligent search capabilities into your partner portal or central content repository.

This goes beyond simple keyword matching. AI-powered semantic search understands the *intent* behind a query. This way, a partner doesn't have to remember the exact file name of a document—they can ask a natural language question like, "What's the best case study to share with a prospect in DACH that is worried about missing tight deployment timelines?"

When the AI tool understands the context—the industry, region, and customer pain points—it can then provide the best document to address their need. This simple application of AI can dramatically reduce friction and increase the utilization of your enablement content.

Leading sales enablement platforms, which are often extended to partners, excel here. **Highspot** uses semantic search to make content discovery intuitive, and **Showpad**'s "AI-Powered Answers in Search" synthesizes information from multiple documents to provide a direct answer to a partner's question, not just a list of links. **Seismic**'s Aura AI offers similar powerful, context-aware search capabilities to ensure partners self-serve effectively.

Level 2: Advanced

At the advanced level, partners might be offered access to an AI-based avatar to role-play their next sales call and provide instant, objective feedback on their performance—continuing to practice and refine their interaction until the partner feels confident and competent.

Vendors like **Second Nature, Mindtickle,** and **Allego** are leaders in this space, offering highly realistic sales simulations that can be customized with your company's products, messaging, and common sales scenarios, making them worth considering for partner training.

Level 3: AI-Enabled

At the AI-enabled stage of partner support is a virtual "coseller" experience—one in which your enablement system isn't waiting for the partner to ask for help, but is providing it proactively.

This involves using AI to understand the context of what a partner is working on and then push relevant content and training to them. It also involves providing scalable, on-demand opportunities for partners to practice and hone their skills.

By seeding your enablement platform with your sales best practices, the AI can analyze the details of a partner-managed opportunity—its sales stage, the prospect's industry, the products being discussed, and any logged competitors. Based on this context, it can automatically surface a playbook of recommended content to assist the partner.

For example, if a prospect in the financial services sector has started asking questions about a particular competitor, the agent might push the relevant competitive battle card, a case study of a large bank that chose your product over that competitor, and an ROI calculator prepopulated with publicly available data about their assets under management, number of employees, or other relevant context. Going one step further, a personalized email may be drafted on your partner's behalf to share relevant insights with their prospects.

Gong, Clari Copilot, and **Outreach** already provide a lot of these capabilities to team members in your sales organization. The strategic play for a CRO is to explore how to extend licenses or integrate these powerful capabilities into your partner program, effectively giving every partner a world-class sales coach on every call.

Offering this level of support can be a major differentiator for your company—identifying you as one of the easiest and most effective partners. At the same time, your governance council will want to be sure rigorous data quality processes are in place—and that real humans are involved in the final approval of important messaging or commitments.

Should your AI tool hallucinate and assist your partner in promising a product, capability, or contractual obligation that you're not prepared to fulfill, you not only may lose credibility with them, but you may also incur significant legal liability.

CO-SELLING AND LEAD MANAGEMENT

The operational mechanics of managing a channel—deal registration, lead routing, territory assignments, and conflict resolution—have historically been an administrative challenge that consumes a lot of your partner account manager's time and frustrates your channel partners, too.

These are the kinds of tasks that might also logically be delegated to AI as the lowest-cost resource capable of doing the job. AI tools become even more exciting when they help you bridge the gap between what your CRM data tells you and what your partner's systems know—creating a shared intelligence that drives more predictable revenue for everyone.

Level 1: Foundational

The first step is to get your operational house in order by automating the basic, rules-based processes for lead management and deal registration. This foundational level of sophistication uses the engines in your PRM or CRM systems to handle the high volume of routine tasks that don't require human judgment.

You can establish simple "if-then" rules to manage these processes. For example, "IF a partner submits a deal registration for a net-new logo with a value less than $10,000 and there is no existing open opportunity for that account, THEN automatically approve the registration and notify the partner."

This foundational level of automation cleans up the administrative noise, ensures faster response times for partners, and frees your channel team from mundane data entry tasks. Nearly all modern PRM platforms, including **Impartner, ZINFI,** and **Mindmatrix,** provide robust workflow automation to handle these tasks. The native automation capabilities in CRM systems like **HubSpot** can also be configured to manage these basic partner workflows.

Level 2: Advanced

At the advanced level, you move from simple rules-based automation to data-driven intelligence. This involves using AI for predictive analysis and—more exciting—leveraging data sharing to see beyond your own four walls.

First, AI tools can be applied to score and prioritize the leads submitted by partners. Instead of treating every lead equally, the tool might analyze the demographic and behavioral data associated with each lead, comparing them to your previous won and lost deals. Then, it might assign a predictive score, indicating the lead's likelihood to convert, allowing your team and partners to focus their efforts on the opportunities with the highest probability of success.

PRM tools like **Journeybee** offer this capability, using AI features to score and prioritize partner-submitted leads based on historical close rates.

Even more powerfully, at this stage in your AI journey, you might introduce a platform that securely connects your CRM systems and maps your account, lead, and opportunity data.

This integration promises to allow you to see a list of all your open opportunities where one of your partners already has an established customer relationship—moving co-selling from a hopeful guessing game to a precise, data-driven strategy. **Crossbeam** is a leader in this space, and platforms like **Partner Fleet** can integrate these signals directly into a partner marketplace, highlighting co-sell opportunities for partners as they browse.

Level 3: AI-Enabled

The most sophisticated organizations won't just use ecosystem data to identify co-sell opportunities; they'll deploy AI agents to proactively orchestrate the co-selling motion directly within their sellers' and partners' daily workflows.

Consider an AI agent that lives inside your seller's CRM instance that constantly monitors their pipeline for signals of risk or opportunity. When it detects a deal that has stalled for two weeks, it automatically queries your ecosystem intelligence platform. It discovers that while your deal is stuck, one of your key technology partners just closed a new deal with the CFO at that same account last month.

In an AI-enabled process, the AI agent wouldn't just surface this information on a dashboard—it would take action by sending your seller a Slack message: "Your opportunity with LuminaCore has not progressed in three weeks. Our partner has a strong, recent relationship with the economic buyer. Call Andrea Davis for a warm introduction." The agent might even provide a prewritten, personalized email template to use in making that outreach.

AI-enabling the partner ecosystem in this way would involve synthesizing the capabilities of many of the tools already discussed, including **Crossbeam** Copilot, **Salesforce, HubSpot**, and conversational intelligence platforms like **Gong**.

As you consider using AI to collaborate with partners for these Level 2 and Level 3 use cases, you'll want to pay particular attention to data privacy, ethical, and legal risks, however.

Sharing raw CRM data with partners (even "trusted" ones with confidentiality agreements in place) can trigger risks related to price fixing, violations of antitrust laws, or GDPR/CCPA concerns related to "third-party sharing" consent that was not properly obtained.

To mitigate these concerns, your governance team will want to carefully examine your technologies' abilities to use "data clean rooms" to identify mutual opportunities for collaboration without either party ever seeing the other's raw customer list, personally identifiable information, or other protected data.

SIZING THE CUSTOMER RENEWAL PIE

As the CRO sets a revenue plan for their company, they're not just looking for the new logo deals their direct sales teams and partners can generate. High-growth plans are also often built on the high potential of renewals, price increases, and product expansion within existing accounts.

Conversely, because recurring revenue can be such a significant portion of annual billings, customer churn can quickly derail the annual plan.

AI provides the sales leader with a number of capabilities to strategically think about this part of their business and create sensible annual revenue plans.

Level 1: Foundational

Sales organizations can find a great roadmap to available install-base revenues by examining the contracts they have with each customer. These documents typically tell you everything you need to know about when the customer is up for renewal, how much flexibility the customer has to increase or decrease usage, notification periods for cancellation, and what price increase is pre-agreed or permissible.

Yet many sales organizations struggle to manage this analysis in a structured way because they've had different standard contract terms at different points in their history, and the details have been customized for individual customers to win different deals.

Creating a bottom-up forecast of customer renewal revenues, then, can be a time-consuming, manual process that involves reading hundreds or thousands of PDFs stored in digital archives. Often, pre-negotiated price escalators aren't applied, or auto-renewal windows are missed, creating costly last-minute negotiations with existing accounts.

A variety of off-the-shelf contract lifecycle management platforms—including **Sirion, Malbek,** and **Icertis**—use AI to address this challenge by using natural language processing to identify, extract, and structure key contract terms, organizing them into a reportable database that can then be queried to create a forecast of secured, up-for-renewal, and at-risk customer revenues in the coming year.

Level 2: Advanced

Beyond these basic capabilities, AI tools can also flag nonstandard or high-risk clauses by comparing each contract's text against the company's current legal standard. For example, contracts with unlimited liability or "termination for convenience" language might be flagged, allowing you to build a strategy for which terms you might want to renegotiate at the next renewal, how much price increase you may want to forgo to secure them, and what the implication of those choices would be for the overall book of business in the coming year.

Platforms like **Legartis** and **GEP Smart** help provide market trends alongside AI insights from your own contract set to assist with this.

SETTING EXPECTATIONS BASED ON CUSTOMER INSIGHTS

Analyzing contracts in this way is helpful—but it just provides an upper-end estimate of the revenue that can possibly come from existing customers in the coming year. Some customers will go out of business, while others will be unhappy with your service and choose to terminate their agreements, and customer success platforms use AI to help set appropriate expectations.

For many organizations, a customer success manager—if there are any—or an account manager assigns a red/yellow/green status to customers based on their subjective understanding of the account, which can feed into your expectations.

Level 2: Advanced

In addition to these human judgment-based insights, AI tools are increasingly able to identify patterns in structured data systems that might be helpful in predicting a customer's propensity to churn. **Gainsight** is a frequently recognized leader in this space. **ChurnZero, Catalyst** (now part of Totango), **and AppEQ** are also well-regarded players, and even CRM players like **Salesforce** are embedding these capabilities into their core platforms with tools like Einstein.

These systems often look to predictors like:

- **Product usage data.** A basic application of usage data might identify trends of increasing or decreasing logins to your solution as an indicator of customer usage. At a more granular level, you might explore whether key features within your product are being used—learning over time that certain feature sets lead to a high level of "product stickiness," while a lack of adoption tends to raise churn risk.

- **Support ticket data.** Total volume of support tickets is a key place to start, and looking at the severity and resolution time can provide additional levels of insight. Increasingly, sentiment analysis from call recordings, email exchanges, or post-support surveys is helping to inform churn risk.

- **Engagement data.** Here, systems look to see if customers are attending webinars, opening emails, responding to NPS surveys, or showing other signs of engagement to feed the customer health score.

- **Financial data.** Accounts that are consistently late in payments may be experiencing financial distress or dissatisfaction that leads to churn.

- **News data.** Unstructured data—such as a press release announcing the departure of your key champion from the organization, or an announcement of large layoffs in the departments that use your product—might also be used to create an assessment of customer health.

AI synthesizes these data points into a unified health score, providing a more accurate foundation for next year's revenue projection. Rather than broad guesses, these systems produce account-level predictions such as "This account has an 82% likelihood of churning when their contract is up in June," based on patterns identified across thousands of similar accounts.

With this insight, you can build a revenue plan that assumes the churn happens and have a more realistic annual plan as a result.

Level 3: AI-Enabled

Ideally, you also use these insights to identify key accounts where you might deploy additional resources (to resolve tickets faster, encourage adoption of key features, or build a stronger rapport with a new leader) to improve your upside potential. When your system evolves from simply flagging account risk to recommending a specific course of action to you, you've moved into the AI-enabled level of sophistication.

Here, AI tools help prioritize a CSM's day with a set of prioritized tasks informed by data-driven insights.

PLANNING CROSS-SELL

Beyond simply renewing existing contracts, most sales organizations also plan to sell additional products to their install base—leading to a net retention rate above 100%.

Level 1: Foundational

To achieve this goal, sales teams first need to conduct a whitespace analysis—essentially a spreadsheet grid listing each customer as a row, each product as a column, and the cell intersections as indicators of the size of the opportunity for unsold products.

Many of the contract lifecycle management products discussed for identifying price increase and renewal data can also be used to create this report, and solutions like **DemandFarm, Revegy,** and **ARPEDIA** also offer functionality targeted for this need.

Level 2: Advanced

While current whitespace analysis tools can help you plan which products to pitch to which customers today, a more advanced approach may turn to conversational intelligence tools (like **Gong, Chorus.ai,** or **Clari Copilot**) to uncover needs for future product development.

Here, you'll want your system to look for comments like "I really wish that your product could do X," or conversations about new strategic initiatives that might be filtered and presented to your product development teams as part of the annual planning process with an assessment that "if we could offer this feature set, it would be worth this amount of revenue from these customers that have already indicated an interest for it."

Level 3: AI-Enabled

Much like the new logo motion, integrating intent data for your existing customers can be beneficial. Sourcing it from platforms such as **6sense, Cognism/Bombora, Demandbase,** or **ZoomInfo** might show that multiple employees from your accounts are researching topics related to your products.

When you combine that with automated outreach tools like **Clay, HubSpot, Outreach,** or **Salesloft,** you can develop a fully AI-enabled process. Here, an agent might identify the customer's research activity and queue up a personalized email on the account manager's behalf to invite their account to a webinar on the topic or suggest getting together to introduce the relevant product offering.

EMPOWERING CUSTOMER SUCCESS

Much of the analysis used to predict customer churn will also be helpful to customer success managers, who may or may not have revenue targets that make it into the annual plan.

The fully AI-enabled organization may also decide that it's not economically viable to assign a human CSM to every customer, while still agreeing they don't want to leave a long tail of customers completely underserved.

In such organizations, autonomous AI agents might be deployed to manage these less-profitable segments at scale. AI-powered CS agents might execute entire workflows—providing automated onboarding sequences, sending proactive, AI-generated check-in emails based on usage patterns, and offering intelligent, context-aware support.

For example, if a customer's usage of a key feature drops, the AI tool might simultaneously trigger three actions:

1. Send a personalized email from the marketing automation platform with a link to a tutorial on that feature.
2. Create a low-priority task for the CSM to check in on their next call.
3. Surface an in-app guide the next time the user logs in.

This use of AI moves beyond simple automation to predictive, real-time orchestration of the entire customer experience. It ensures that all customers receive a baseline level of proactive engagement while allowing the human CSMs to dedicate their expertise exclusively to the most strategic, high-value accounts.

Expanding your customer success operations with AI creates powerful opportunities, but your governance council will also need to mitigate the same customer trust, data privacy, and legal liability risks we've explored with other customer-facing uses of AI bots.

As established in our accountability framework, the organization still remains the fiduciary for every bot-led interaction and will be held liable for promises and advice given, whether hallucinated or not.

If you deploy autonomous agents for the "long tail" of your business, you'll also want to ensure efficiency doesn't come at the cost of the customer relationship. If one of these customers realizes they're the only ones not getting a human CSM, will it accelerate their churn? Disclosing the non-human nature of their interactions—with some path to connect with a human when necessary—may be a key part of this strategy.

ANNUAL PLANNING

When we bring together the new logo acquisition, account renewal activities, and install base cross-sell motions, we can craft a comprehensive annual plan for the sales year.

I'm a fan of consolidating this into a "one-page plan" that can be used with the board, the c-team, and every sales leader to ensure everyone understands what is expected to happen and when.

As shown in Figure 2, it is a simple grid that identifies the various sources of revenue and maps revenue targets by month based on an understanding of historical seasonal performance. Additionally, it provides channel-level pipeline requirements that are informed by sales velocity insights so that a team that closes 25% of its pipeline in 60 days, for example, requires four times its revenue target to be generated in the pipeline two months ahead of time.

In 000's

Bookings By Team By Month

	JAN	FEB	MAR	APR	MAY	JUN	JUL	AUG	SEPT	OCT	NOV	DEC	TOTAL
Enterprise New Logo	0.15552	0.23328	0.3888	0.171072	0.256608	0.42768	0.171072	0.256608	0.42768	0.279936	0.419904	0.69984	3.888
SMB New Logo	0.0864	0.1296	0.216	0.09504	0.14256	0.2376	0.09504	0.14256	0.2376	0.15552	0.23328	0.3888	2.16
Cross-sell Install Base	0.10368	0.15552	0.2592	0.114048	0.171072	0.28512	0.114048	0.171072	0.28512	0.186624	0.279936	0.46656	2.592
Renewal and Price Increases	1.3824	2.0736	3.456	1.52064	2.28096	3.8016	1.52064	2.28096	3.8016	2.48832	3.73248	6.2208	34.56
New Assumption: New Product Launch/Sales						0.045	0.075	0.125	0.3	0.366	0.366	0.415	1.692
New Assumption: Expanded Team/Hires					0.121	0.172	0.06	0.095	0.158	0.082	0.281	0.298	1.267
New Assumption: Sales Training Improvements		0.002333	0.011664	0.051322	0.076982	0.128304	0.051322	0.076982	0.128304	0.083981	0.125971	0.209952	0.947117
Total Bookings	1.728	2.594333	4.331664	1.952122	3.049182	5.097304	2.087122	3.148182	5.338304	3.642381	5.438571	8.698952	47.10612

In 000's

Pipeline Needed By Team By Month

	JAN	FEB	MAR	APR	MAY	JUN	JUL	AUG	SEPT	OCT	NOV	DEC	TOTAL
Sr. New Logo	0.5346	0.8019	1.3365	0.8748	1.3122	2.187	12.15						19.197
Jr New Logo	0.327724	0.491586	0.81931	0.327724	0.491586	0.81931	0.536276	0.804414	1.34069	7.448276			13.4069
Install Base	0.324	0.14256	0.21384	0.3564	0.14256	0.21384	0.3564	0.23328	0.34992	0.5832	3.24		6.156
New Product Pipeline				0.225	0.375	0.625	1.5	1.83	1.83	2.075			8.46
New Hire Pipeline	0.484	0.688	0.24	0.38	0.632	0.328	1.124	1.192					5.068
Total Pipeline Created	1.186324	1.436046	2.36965	1.783924	2.321346	3.84515	14.54268	2.867694	3.52061	10.10648	3.24		52.2879

Figure 2: A Sample One-Page Plan

Level 2: Advanced

The forecasting functionality previously discussed in revenue intelligence platforms like **Clari, Outreach, Gong,** or **Salesloft** can help in this process, giving you a team-by-team breakdown of win rates, deal cycle lengths, average deal sizes, and more.

Level 3: AI-Enabled

I also recommend breaking out speculative revenue sources for which no data exists.

Perhaps we're planning to launch a new product halfway through the year, but we don't yet know the win rate or average deal size. Or maybe we're making a bet that a new sales training program will improve conversion rates by 1% in the first month, 2% in the second, and 3% thereafter.

These assumptions are often based on gut feel, and breaking them out as distinct parts of the chart help us have conversations throughout the year like "We assumed our new training program would have a 3% increase in win rate, but we're actually seeing 7%" or "The three-month delay associated with being late on our product roadmap puts $1.1M of potential revenue at risk this year."

AI tools can help us move past this guesswork by simulating scenarios using tools like **Anaplan** or **Jedox** to model different ramp periods, pricing models, and other variables when creating our plans. We might get an even better plan when we engage in continuous modeling throughout the year—incorporating up-to-date market trends, sales capacity, and current win rates into the analysis.

IN SUM

For the modern sales leader, AI offers a powerful ability to escape the limitations of point-in-time data and instead build a dynamic, forward-looking revenue strategy. Whether through TAM analysis, partner enablement, or customer churn planning, AI tools enable the CRO to continuously monitor their ecosystem and adapt plans in real time.

These tools elevate the CRO's strategic profile, helping them shift from merely reporting a reliable number to the board to actively architecting the desired revenue outcome through scenario planning at scale.

The following table summarizes the discussed applications of AI for the modern CRO. Use it to evaluate your existing revenue engine, prioritize the high-impact AI transitions that support your goals, and refine your shortlist of strategic technology partners.

Process Stage	Specific Task	AI Application	Example Vendors/Products
TAM Analysis for New Logo Motions	TAM/SAM/SOM definition	Use generative AI to review and synthesize market reports to estimate market size.	ChatGPT, Gemini, Claude
	Bottom-up account list creation & prioritization	Use packaged data providers for account lists and augment with intent data for prioritization.	ZoomInfo, Cognism, Apollo.io, 6sense, Demandbase
	Identifying new customer segments	Analyze internal data (calls, emails, CRM) to identify non-obvious customer segments.	Gong (Data Cloud), CRM tools, email systems
	Continuous market analysis	Deploy an AI agent to continuously monitor real-time data sources (news, filings, intent) to update target lists.	Gong (Data Cloud), CRM tools, email systems, external data feeds

Process Stage	Specific Task	AI Application	Example Vendors/Products
Partner Identification & Recruitment	Defining ideal partner profile (IPP)	Use generative AI as a brainstorming partner to flesh out a detailed IPP.	ChatGPT, Gemini, Claude
	Generating partner outreach	Prompt generative AI to create personalized, tailored outreach email templates.	ChatGPT, Gemini, Claude
	Smart partner matching	Use specialized platforms to analyze top performers and find "lookalike" partners at scale.	PartnerOptimizer, Mindmatrix BridgeAI
	Autonomous partner recruitment	AI agent continuously scans the market, identifies/scores new partners, and manages initial outreach.	
Partner Enablement (Onboarding)	Automating standard onboarding	Use workflow automation to trigger pre-defined sequences (welcome email, assign tasks, deliver content).	Impartner (Journey Builder), ZINFI (Partner Onboarding Manager), PartnerStack, Datamatics Copilot

Process Stage	Specific Task	AI Application	Example Vendors/Products
	Personalized onboarding curriculum	Analyze partner attributes (type, tier, region) to dynamically assemble a relevant onboarding path.	Journeybee, Mindmatrix, ZINFI
	Adaptive, real-time onboarding	AI agent acts as a "personal tutor" to monitor engagement and dynamically adjust the learning path.	Disco.co, Allego
Partner Enablement (Just-in-Time)	Intelligent content discovery	AI-powered semantic search in a partner portal that understands the intent of natural language questions.	Highspot, Showpad, Seismic (Aura AI)
	Sales call/role-play practice	Offer AI-based avatars for partners to role-play sales calls and receive instant feedback.	Second Nature, Mindtickle, Allego

Process Stage	Specific Task	AI Application	Example Vendors/Products
	Proactive, contextual "co-seller"	AI integrates with CRM, analyzes opportunity context, and proactively pushes a "playbook" or drafts emails.	Gong, Clari Copilot, Outreach
Co-Selling & Lead Management	Automating lead routing & deal registration	Use "if-then" rules in PRM/CRM to automatically handle routine administrative tasks.	Impartner, ZINFI, Mindmatrix, HubSpot
	Predictive lead scoring (partner)	AI models analyze partner-submitted leads and assign a predictive score based on conversion likelihood.	Journeybee
	Identifying co-sell opportunities	Use ecosystem platforms to securely connect CRMs and map account data to find partner overlaps.	Crossbeam, Partner Fleet

Process Stage	Specific Task	AI Application	Example Vendors/Products
Co-Selling & Lead Management	Proactive co-sell orchestration	AI agent monitors stalled deals, queries ecosystem data, and proactively suggests co-sell actions (e.g., via Slack).	Crossbeam Copilot, Salesforce, HubSpot, Gong
Sizing the Customer Renewal Pie	Contract analysis (renewal/pricing terms)	Use NLP in CLM platforms to extract key contract terms (dates, price escalators) into a database.	Sirion, Malbek, Icertis
	Flagging non-standard/ high-risk contracts	Compare contract text against legal standards to flag risks and inform negotiation strategy.	Legartis, GEP Smart
Setting Customer Expectations	Predicting customer churn (health scoring)	Calculate a health score by analyzing product usage, support tickets, engagement, financial data, and news.	Gainsight, ChurnZero, Catalyst (Totango), AppEQ, Salesforce (Einstein)

Process Stage	Specific Task	AI Application	Example Vendors/Products
	Recommending retention actions	AI moves from flagging risk to recommending specific actions and prioritizing a CSM's daily tasks.	
Planning Cross-sell	Whitespace analysis	Use CLM or account planning tools to create a grid of customers vs. products to find unsold opportunities.	CLM platforms, DemandFarm, Revegy, ARPEDIA
	Uncovering future product needs	Use conversational intelligence to analyze calls for customer requests (e.g., "I wish you could do X").	Gong, Chorus.ai, Clari Copilot
	Automated cross-sell outreach	Combine intent data (customer research) with automated outreach tools to queue personalized emails.	6sense, Cognism/Bombora, Demandbase, ZoomInfo, Clay, HubSpot, Outreach, Salesloft

Process Stage	Specific Task	AI Application	Example Vendors/Products
Empowering Customer Success	Managing "long-tail" customers	(AI-Enabled) Deploy autonomous AI agents to manage low-touch segments with automated check-ins, tutorials, and guides.	
Annual Planning	Aggregating sales velocity data	Use revenue intelligence platforms to get team-by-team data (win rates, cycle lengths) for planning.	Clari, Outreach, Gong, Salesloft
	Modeling speculative revenue/scenario planning	Use AI planning tools to simulate scenarios for new products or initiatives and engage in continuous modeling.	Anaplan, Jedox

AI FOR REVENUE OPERATIONS

In the last chapter, we discussed using AI to build an annual plan that sets revenue targets by combining assumptions about each revenue source. With an annual plan set, the next tactical step is to break those targets down into specific instructions for each team member—assigning them an appropriate quota within a prescribed territory and with a prescribed sales playbook to follow to achieve the goal.

Increasingly, organizations have turned to a revenue operations team to lead these tasks—and it's a job that requires a lot of data manipulation and reporting. However, we've missed an important opportunity if we view RevOps solely as data manipulators. They'll add a lot more value to the organization if they're able to use that data to offer strategic or tactical insights on how to improve sales outcomes. RevOps professionals will reclaim time to focus on questions such as "Is our revenue model still accurate?" when they delegate the massive workload of answering "Is our data correct?" to AI tools.

TERRITORY PLANNING

For many RevOps professionals, the start of the fiscal year is preceded by a few hectic weeks of planning seller-focused communications. They wait for the annual plan to be finalized, then spend late nights breaking down targets for an ever-changing number of sellers, assigning what are hopefully fair territories, and mail merging it all into dozens or hundreds of comp plans to be delivered to the sales team on the first day of the new year.

The cost of this manual rush is high. Abacum suggests that in this crush of work, only 39% of organizations effectively integrate important data from core systems such as CRM, ERP, and market intelligence tools, creating serious territory blind spots that can result in unbalanced workloads, missed market opportunities, and, ultimately, unhappy sellers.

There are a few key ways that AI tools have the potential to address these challenges.

Level 1: Foundational

At the foundational level, RevOps needs clean, standardized data to balance opportunity across a number of fair territories. While the CRO identifies the total TAM where the company will be focused, RevOps focuses on the who and the how by slicing it into territories that maximize each seller's chance of success.

The AI features native to CRM platforms like **Salesforce** or **HubSpot** make it easy for RevOps to use metrics such as account counts or lead volume in their work of creating balanced territories.

Level 2: Advanced

At the next level of sophistication, organizations can integrate market intelligence data to identify high-growth, high-opportunities areas that can support additional investment in the selling team. Sales performance management (SPM) platforms like **Anaplan, Varicent,** and **Pigment** help organizations assess a variety of scenarios to see how changes in territories, staffing, and demand might affect the overall revenue plan's likelihood of attainment.

RevOps professionals might also be assisted by tools such as **CARTO,** which provides access to complex location data through natural language chat, allowing territory planners to answer questions like "Where should we deploy our next seller?" or "How do we best balance account potential against the travel time required to cover it?" as they make territory assignments.

Level 3: AI-Enabled

At the fully AI-enabled level, vendors like **Relevance AI** suggest that territory assignments can become truly dynamic. In this use case, teams might not rely on static territory boundaries. Instead, AI agents might continuously monitor territory conditions and sales performance, proactively suggesting strategic adjustments to territory borders and resource allocation to capture maximum opportunity.

Relevance cites, as an example of this model, an Austin-based real estate brokerage that discovered a top-performing agent was spread too thin across three rapidly growing neighborhoods. After redistributing two of those areas to up-and-coming brokers, the agent's total transactions increased 23% in a single quarter.[4]

When considering strategies like this, it's important to recognize that the technology only enables the tactical execution of territory planning—an organization must be culturally aligned with the plan. My experience with the human element of sales organizations is that frequent changes (especially those that result in a loss of territory) are often met with significant resistance, so using AI to continuously, dynamically change territories may not be practical for all sales teams, especially those without team-based quotas.

For organizations that adopt territory changes through Level 3 applications of AI (and even those who have more human intervention in Level 2 approaches), transparency needs to be a key part of the program. As sellers see changes to their territories, they need to understand why the adjustments were made the way they were. A lack of understanding of the inputs that drive AI models may lead to distrust, lack of motivation, and potential lawsuits claiming discriminatory treatment.

---

4 "Free Your Team.Build Your First AI Agent Today!," Territory Manager AI Agents|Relevance AI, accessed January 26, 2026, https://relevanceai.com/agent-templates-roles/territory-manager-ai-agents-1#:~:text=A%20compelling%20case%20study%20comes,31%25%20compared%20to%20control%20regions.

Your governance council will also want to pay attention to the completeness of the data used to inform your territory-building models, keeping an eye out for accidental algorithmic "redlining." Models built from incomplete data—perhaps due to historical coverage or a lack of customer digital presence in key geographies—may lead to incorrect conclusions about the actual business potential in each region. Watch to ensure that these data anomalies are not creating systemic disadvantages for sellers aligned to regions that are poorly represented in the data, but where buying intent is high.

The council will also want to pay attention to contractual obligations you have with your sellers when using AI to shift territory boundaries. In many legal jurisdictions, a sales quota and its assigned territory are viewed as part of a formal employment contract or agreement, and HR and legal will want to consider the impacts on sellers if either component changes.

QUOTA ASSIGNMENT

For many organizations, the easiest approach to quota allocation is one of top-down, even division. Operating from the assumption that every seller has an equal opportunity to succeed, they take the overall company goal, divide it by the number of sellers, add some padding to the results, and assign every seller on the team the same target.

While simple to execute, this approach fails to recognize that even in the best-planned territories, there will be variations in operating conditions. A territory that has been unstaffed for some time may need time to rebuild brand awareness, while a well-established market might be overrun with competition. New hires require time to ramp into the performance levels of their long-tenured peers.

But for a lot of organizations, the only adjustments to these quotas are arbitrary and based on gut-feel, and they're only applied in the territories where there has been a significantly loud complaint about perceived unfairness.

Here, too, SPM platforms such as **Anaplan, Pigment,** and **Varicent** provide advanced, Level 2 capabilities by leveraging AI to model different territory dynamics to inform bottom-up quota assignments. And—just as with using AI for rebalancing territory assignments—the ethical considerations require transparent communication about which factors are used to assign different quotas to different sellers.

Similarly, while agentic AI tools could theoretically be deployed to dynamically suggest mid-period tweaks to sales targets by seller, the cultural and legal risks of moving the finish line mid-race risk making this Level 3 approach a dangerous misfire. As with other use cases we've discussed, the governance council's primary rule must be "the algorithm informs the plan, but human beings make the decision." This maxim might be further informed by the maxim "Just because you can, doesn't mean you should."

COMP PLAN DEVELOPMENT AND COMMUNICATION

Once territories and quotas have been assigned for each seller, they need to be turned into individual compensation plans. Often, plans include accelerated payment rates for higher levels of performance (so the rate I receive at 20% of my quota isn't the same as the one I get at 60, 80, or 100+%, for example).

Additionally, special incentives may be created to induce certain strategic behaviors (earning bonuses for selling more of this product, prioritizing contracts with automatic renewal periods spanning multiple years, etc.).

At the foundational stage, RevOps professionals can use generative AI tools as an intelligent assistant to quickly draft individualized plans that draw from a standard set of components and legal language to implement these goals.

As you consider comp plan components that incentivize behaviors you believe will lead to revenue, it may be natural to gravitate toward easily measurable activities, such as time spent on calls, number of emails sent, and so on.

However, employees may quickly learn to game call durations or send junk emails to win the bonus—even though they don't arrive at the outcome (booked revenue) that you're seeking.

As conversational intelligence tools offer the ability to assess the quality of calls and messages, they may help identify when sellers are "gaming the system" in this way, but your people and culture teams will want to weigh in on unintended consequences of comp plan changes, and your ethics and legal professionals will also need to be consulted as labor surveillance and employee privacy laws evolve.

Level 2: Advanced

Again, the SPM platforms used for advanced territory and quota assignment also often include out-of-the-box features to assemble, disseminate, and receive acknowledgment of each seller's comp plan.

Incentive compensation management platforms like **Forma.ai** or **CaptivateIQ** allow leaders to run detailed simulations of proposed plans to calculate what this year's plan might have paid each seller against last year's performance, and how the payout distribution would have shifted across top, middle, and low performers.

Forma.ai also promotes the use of natural language chat commands to automatically generate plan components, so compensation rules can be built from prompts such as "Create three tiers of payouts that include a 1.5x accelerator for deals over 100% attainment."

When using AI to build comp plan components, it's also important to keep an eye on how the plans operate as a whole. AI tools can be used to flag potential hidden biases—checking, for example, whether a new product SPIFF inadvertently penalizes sellers from lower-potential territories, and promoting fairness and consistency in compensation applications. This functionality is increasingly common in incentive compensation management and HR systems.

Case Study: Accelerating Comp Plan Development with AI

The Challenge: Manual Bottlenecks and "Excel Chaos"

A multinational tech company struggled with territory and quota management processes. Reliance on fragmented, Excel-based blueprints meant multiple revision cycles, coverage gaps, delayed operational readiness, missed goal sheets, and frequent payout adjustments.

The Solution: AI-Assisted Sales Planning

The organization transitioned from disconnected spreadsheets to a centralized, cloud-based planning platform to streamline sales operations for its management users.

- **Unified territory logic:** The company redesigned its territory construction and assignment processes for worldwide consistency, replacing localized manual interventions with a single source of truth.

- **Dynamic quota modeling:** The new system helped the company define monthly quota values based on market seasonality and specific employee ramping schedules, ensuring more equitable and accurate targets.

- **Automated guardrails:** By implementing data guardrails and automated approval workflows, the organization enabled sales management to identify coverage scenario values and account movements in real time.

The ROI: Enhanced Speed and Precision

- **Rapid operational readiness:** The transition led to the on-time delivery of goal sheets to the field and significantly reduced the time taken in territory updates.

> - **De-risked GTM execution:** The company eliminated productivity dips by identifying coverage gaps and territory changes before they impacted sales performance.
> - **Data-driven decision-making:** Leadership gained immediate visibility into territory viability and profitability metrics, allowing for more informed decisions on equitable account assignments.

Level 3: AI-Enabled

Once plans are communicated, AI tools can act as on-demand coaches for sellers. This ensures immediate support at any hour while freeing RevOps analysts from repetitive administrative queries.

For example, **CaptivateIQ** Assist is a "payee coach" that allows sellers to ask natural-language questions about their performance and potential earnings. A seller might ask, "What is the financial benefit of me offering a 10% discount to pull this deal forward three weeks vs. letting it close naturally next quarter?" and receive an instant, accurate answer.

Organizations will have fundamentally transformed their culture through AI when they use the same insights to push messages to sellers, sending emails or texts that proactively tell them things like "You will earn an additional 2% commission by reaching the next accelerator tier, which is just $500 of bookings away. Closing the VoltaStream deal this week could net you an additional $1,272 in commission."

Similarly, we can imagine an integrated set of agents that monitor real-time performance, assess the best way to get to plan, and proactively suggest end-of-quarter SPIFFs for certain behaviors that unlock the right deals to get the team past their revenue goal.

Extending the logic even further, custom SPIFFs could also be developed in real time by an AI agent that constantly monitors performance against plan. Seeing that the company is missing its quarterly sales goal of a new product, it might identify prospects in the product's ICP that have not been introduced to the solution, and then offer the relevant sellers a personal SPIFF incentive to sell the product to those prospects, while crafting different SPIFFs for other sellers who have different kinds of untapped opportunities in their territories that would advance the company's overall objectives.

Here, too, your governance council's HR and legal representatives will need to weigh in on what's appropriate—offering one seller a $1,000 bonus for closing a specific deal in the desperate last days of the quarter while offering another seller only $500 (or no bonus at all) when they closed a similar deal weeks earlier would expose a cultural and legal landmine.

As the RevOps team increasingly becomes responsible for the management and usage of AI tools, they'll also want to work with the council to carefully consider data integrity and collaborate cross-functionally with finance and other teams to keep refreshing their models.

Over time, AI models degrade, and a forecasting model trained on the high-growth trends in one year's legacy data might be irrelevant when an economic slowdown happens a few years later.

The ability to regularly test the reliability of an AI tool's output and retrain on new trends is a critical technical MLOps competency that many RevOps professionals don't yet have. Because it will only become more urgent, your governance council, HR, and strategy teams will need to figure out how to develop this new capability within your workforce.

MONITORING FOR REVENUE LEAKAGE AND CONTRACT ENFORCEMENT

While territory and quota planning focus on the potential of the revenue engine, the work that RevOps does to monitor contract enforcement focuses on the integrity of the final result. One of the most persistent sources of revenue leakage occurs between what was agreed on in the contract and what was actually invoiced, with missed price increases, unauthorized discounts, or customers who use more licenses than they're paying for as common culprits.

Historically, finding these discrepancies has meant conducting a manual, line-by-line reconciliation of CRM records against contracts—a task so large it happens only occasionally, or only against a small fraction of the total account base.

AI tools, however, offer the opportunity to turn this into a continuous, enterprise-wide search for leaked revenue.

Level 1: Foundational

At the foundational level, RevOps uses generative AI tools as a contract analyst to extract key terms from unstructured documents. Instead of reading through a 35-page Master Services Agreement to find the allowed percentage for annual price increase, they might feed the document into an LLM like **ChatGPT** or **Gemini** to produce an instant summary of relevant contract terms.

Level 2: Advanced

At the advanced level, organizations deploy specialized contract lifecycle management (CLM) platforms such as **Sirion, Malbek,** or **Icertis** to extract key contract terms and flag potential revenue leakage risks through natural language processing.

For example, an AI tool might automatically compare a newly signed contract against the company's standard terms to identify special payment terms or discounts that were added during negotiation, flagging them as risks to give special attention to during the life of the contract.

Level 3: AI-Enabled

At the fully enabled level, AI agents might provide autonomous reconciliation of contract and billing terms—continuously orchestrating work between the CRM system, the contract management system, and the billing system to ensure they're in synch.

For example, an agent might note that a customer's actual product usage has exceeded their contracted limit by 7%. Instead of waiting for a manual end-of-year audit that may never come, the agent might independently verify the "true up" language in that customer's contract, notify the account manager to begin a customer conversation, and draft an email to the customer that documents the overage and includes an invoice for the appropriate amount due.

As has been covered elsewhere, your governance council will want to ensure that a human is in the loop on this process, perhaps requiring the account manager to send the communications and invoice after manually reviewing the contract themselves to ensure that all is correct.

IN SUM

The RevOps professional's job has often been dominated by a heavy, manual workload of data manipulation—especially during the year-end job of annual planning, comp plan, and territory design. This burden typically relegates the role to a reactive one where professionals spend their time fixing spreadsheets, rather than fixing the business.

Because of its ability to manage large sets of data and identify patterns, AI can fundamentally assist RevOps in each of these functions. It also gives them the time to move from asking "Is this spreadsheet correct?" to questions like "Is this incentive structure driving the right behavior?" In doing so, they can elevate their role to one of a strategic partner to the GTM leadership team.

This table summarizes AI opportunities for the RevOps professional. Leverage it to assess your data readiness for advanced modeling, identify specific process bottlenecks ripe for automation, and select the tools that will transform your role from manual data processor to strategic business partner.

Process Stage	Specific Task	AI Application	Example Vendors/ Products
Territory Planning	Balancing territories	Use native AI features to balance territories based on metrics (e.g., account count, lead volume).	Salesforce, HubSpot
	Integrating market intelligence	Assess various scenarios (changes in territory, staffing, demand) to see the effects on the revenue goal.	Anaplan, Varicent, Pigment
	Accessing location data	Use natural language chat to answer questions about seller deployment and travel time.	CARTO
	Dynamic territory assignment	AI agents continuously monitor conditions and performance, proactively suggesting strategic adjustments.	Relevance AI
Quota Assignment	Informing bottom-up quotas	Leverage AI to model different territory dynamics.	Anaplan, Pigment, Varicent
Comp Plan Development & Communication	Drafting individualized plans	Use generative AI as an intelligent assistant to draft plans from standard components and legal language.	

Process Stage	Specific Task	AI Application	Example Vendors/ Products
	Assembling & disseminating plans	Use out-of-the-box features in SPM platforms for plan management.	Anaplan, Varicent, Pigment
	Simulating proposed plans	Run detailed simulations (e.g., against last year's performance) to see payout distribution.	Forma.ai, CaptivateIQ
	Building plan components	Use natural language chat commands to automatically generate plan components (e.g., payout tiers).	Forma.ai
	Assessing plans for fairness	Assess plans to flag potential hidden biases and ensure fairness and consistency.	ICM and HR systems
	Answering seller questions	Provide an on-demand "comp plan coach" ("Payee Coach") to answer natural language questions.	CaptivateIQ (Assist)
	Proactive seller communication	Proactively send messages (email/text) to sellers about potential earnings from specific actions.	

Process Stage	Specific Task	AI Application	Example Vendors/ Products
	Developing custom, real-time SPIFFs	AI agent monitors performance, identifies untapped opportunities, and offers personalized, real-time SPIFFs for individuals and teams.	
Monitoring Revenue Leakage & Contract Enforcement	Extracting commercial terms from unstructured contracts	Use AI to summarize dates, dollars, and notification periods from contract documents.	Sirion, Malbek, Icertis, ChatGPT, Gemini
	Identifying non-standard legal or financial risks	Flag non-standard contract terms for special processing and monitoring	Sirion, Malbek, Icertis
	Real-time usage and billing reconciliation	Autonomous agents that monitor product usage and trigger true-up invoices with AE involvement	Custom integration

AI FOR SALES ENABLEMENT

Creating an annual plan and assigning territories and quotas to support it set the foundation for a successful sales year, but the plan won't be achieved until every member of the go-to-market team understands their role in advancing the plan, is trained and enabled to do their part, and knows how to collaborate with other team members effectively.

SALES PLAYBOOKS

For many organizations, the sales playbook is a published document that becomes the centerpiece of this kind of training.

Level 1: Foundational

At the foundational level, generative AI tools can ingest reports about TAM, ICP, product capabilities, and the job descriptions of sellers, SDRs, and marketers to assemble a playbook that defines the various tasks for lead generation, executing discovery calls, running demos, negotiating contracts, and other typical parts of a seller's day.

Going a step further, AI engines might also be prompted to interview key leaders over a few days or weeks, asking questions about important customer stories, how difficult customer challenges were resolved, and other prompts to refine a hyper-specific playbook for the individual company.

Once published, the same tools can be deployed as a chatbot coach for sellers, who can be consulted for advice based on the latest understanding of the playbook.

A prompt like "Please help me prepare for a demonstration with a mid-tier bank, which is currently using this competitor's offering …" might be responded to with a playbook-approved meeting agenda, stories to tell, and other materials that will equip the seller for their next interactions.

Beyond just creating sales playbooks, I'm increasingly turning to this application of AI whenever sellers or leaders have offered up their resignations—suggesting that they use their two-week notice period to engage in this sort of AI-led interview to capture any specific knowledge their successor would benefit from—and to create a virtual chatbot coach that colleagues can engage with when the employee has long departed the role.

When using LLMs in this way, you'll want your IT and data governance teams to weigh in on the specific tool to use—steering away from public systems that don't have "zero data retention" policies in place.

In doing so, you'll protect your confidential IP, ensuring that public data models aren't getting trained on your confidential and proprietary information (or that of your customers, which may have additional legally enforced protections required for handling).

You'll also want to work closely with HR and legal teams to make sure you're complying with employment agreements and any "right to be forgotten" obligations you have to your existing employees.

Level 2: Advanced

Beyond the generative tools like **ChatGPT** and **Gemini**, category-specific vendors like **PlaybookBuilder.ai, Waybook,** and **Flight** generate playbook documents, answer real-time questions, and

Case Study: Rapid Knowledge Transfer During Post-Merger Integration

The Challenge

Following the acquisition of a niche solution provider, the high-growth acquirer faced a critical risk: the departing sales leader of the acquired firm held the entire GTM "blueprint" in their head.

The company had a few months before the leader's planned departure to extract and document a decade's worth of institutional knowledge, product positioning, and sales processes.

The Solution: The AI-Driven Knowledge Extraction Sprint

The departing leader used a "synthetic consultant" model to condense years of experience into a structured, 240-page sales playbook in just three weeks.

- **SME-to-AI dictation:** The company tasked an AI with interviewing the leader through a series of deep-dive knowledge-transfer sessions. The leader provided verbal "data dumps" via text-to-speech, which the AI immediately synthesized into professional, formatted chapters on buyer personas, deal stages, and competitive positioning.

- **Rapid cross-pollination:** The AI tool was also asked to identify gaps in logic between the acquired company's sales motion and the acquirer's existing framework. This allowed the departing leader to address integration friction points in the playbook before they became operational issues.

- **The "legacy" assistant:** To ensure the knowledge remained accessible after his departure, the leader used the playbook's data to train a custom AI model that could be asked questions in the future.

> **The ROI**
>
> - **90% faster knowledge transfer:** The documentation of a comprehensive, 240-page GTM strategy was completed in **three weeks**, ensuring knowledge was captured before the leader's departure.
>
> - **De-risked integration:** The company successfully avoided the productivity dip typical in acquisitions, as new sellers had a materially complete guide and an AI assistant to navigate the transition.
>
> - **Instant scalability:** The "no-budget" approach saved tens of thousands in consultant fees while providing a higher-fidelity asset than traditional documentation methods.

offer insights as virtual team members trained on your specific data, processes, and language.

When playbooks are integrated with other systems in the ecosystem, they evolve from point-in-time static documents to dynamic ones that manage, activate, and evolve the plays when they're needed most.

We've discussed how tools like **Highspot, Seismic,** and **Spekit** offer real-time coaching to sellers and can push playbook snippets and definitions to them when needed.

Bringing conversational intelligence tools like **Gong** and **Chorus** into the mix, an integrated system might periodically analyze sales calls and emails to see which plays are being used most often—as well as what top sellers are doing that's not in the playbook—and offer up revisions to the playbook based on these insights.

Level 3: AI-Enabled

While a lot of value comes from enforcing compliance with an approved sales playbook, a fully AI-enabled organization may use its tools to continually evolve the playbook in real time.

Case Study: Optimizing Global Methodology via Automated Skill Gap Analysis

The Challenge

A global tech-enabled services organization, formed through the consolidation of three distinct companies across the UK and the US, struggled with fragmented sales cultures and inconsistent execution. Despite similar offerings, each legacy team used different selling styles, leading to unpredictable outcomes and a diluted market presence. The organization needed to institutionalize a unified sales playbook and identify specific skill gaps that varied by region without relying on manual, anecdotal manager feedback.

The Solution: Data-Driven Methodology Alignment

The company established a centralized sales enablement team that used conversational intelligence to audit playbook adoption and provide targeted, regionalized micro-training.

- **Automated methodology auditing:** Using conversational intelligence tools, the company performed monthly assessments of every recorded call to identify uptake of different components of the sales methodology.

- **Targeted global micro-training:** The data revealed a universal struggle: a global failure to identify "power" (economic decision-makers). In response, the following month's global training efforts were focused exclusively on this part of the playbook.

- **Regionalized performance diagnostics:** The analysis also uncovered distinct regional trends: US teams struggled with the paper process, while UK teams struggled with ROI calculation. This enabled the deployment of regional training that addressed the specific weaknesses of each team without wasting time on those who had already mastered the skill.

- **Crowdsourced "best-in-class" libraries:** To drive engagement, the company created a competition that asked sellers to submit a snippet the next month of their best call where they were seeking power. The top three sellers received small cash bonuses, and their call snippets were embedded into the training curriculum, ensuring the methodology was taught using peer-led, real-world examples.

The ROI

- **7% increase in win rates:** By shifting from generic training to data-backed, tactical adjustments, the organization saw a measurable lift in closed-won business across all regions.

- **Unified global brand identity:** By standardizing the sales approach through a single playbook and monitoring its execution, the company successfully moved away from the fragmented "three-company" legacy. This ensured a consistent brand experience for customers regardless of their geographic location or the legacy background of their account executive.

- **Elimination of training waste:** Enablement resources were no longer spent on broad topics the team had already mastered, but were instead focused on the specific skills driving the most friction.

For example, when a particular competitor starts being mentioned with increasing frequency on sales calls, an AI agent might be triggered to scrape the web for their latest press releases and product updates, analyze recent win/loss data against that specific competitor, and review call transcriptions from other deals where they were mentioned.

The tool might then synthesize this information to generate and deploy an up-to-the-minute battle card with recommended talk tracks, differentiation points, and landmines to avoid.

While this use case is not yet a common, off-the-shelf feature in sales tools today, it might be built using platforms like **Beam.ai** to orchestrate a workflow that combines data enrichment providers with generative AI models, CRM data, and your revenue intelligence platform.

As has been covered elsewhere in this book, you'll want to pay careful attention to data integrity—and implement processes to test for hallucinating AI tools that coach sellers incorrectly. It would certainly be ineffective for sellers to follow incorrect advice—and if they're publicly telling prospects or customers about a made-up weakness in a competitor's toolset that is incorrect, they may be opening your company up to liability for misrepresentation.

To mitigate these concerns, consider a process that puts a real human in the approval loop—preventing AI-generated content from being added to the enablement library or given to sellers without a live subject matter expert's sign-off.

CERTIFICATION MANAGEMENT

In earlier chapters, we've reviewed the potential for AI tools to support training and certification of individual sellers (in the Frontline Manager chapter) and partner resources (in the CRO chapter). Organizations with formal sales enablement or training teams, however, will find that these are the professionals who implement such use cases.

Whoever the leader is, they'll find that the promise of AI-driven certification is to shift from traditional learning models where sellers simply watch a series of videos to achieve certification to a continuous enablement model that incorporates personalized, ongoing performance-based feedback to assist every seller in maximizing their potential.

As you shift to these adaptive learning paths, the governance council will need to continue to pay attention to the fine line between "AI-recommended actions" and "digital management" of your teams. Automated employment decisions pose serious legal, ethical, and cultural risks, and you will want to be sure that a live person is ultimately making the high-stakes decisions regarding an employee's career path or certification status.

IN SUM

For years, the sales playbook has been the north star guiding sales and marketing in their collaborative pursuit of the market. However, as markets shift and competitors evolve their offerings, these static documents can quickly become obsolete.

In this chapter, we explored how AI can impact the creation, activation, and evolution of these playbooks more frequently or in real time.

Use this summary to benchmark your transition toward real-time playbook evolution, audit your current training paths for adaptive intelligence, and select the technology partners capable of maintaining your team's competitive edge in a shifting market.

Process Stage	Specific Task	AI Application	Example Vendors/Products
Playbook Creation	Drafting Content	The AI interview: Prompting generative AI to interview leaders and draft playbook sections based on their spoken answers.	ChatGPT, Gemini
	Capturing Tribal Knowledge	Exit interviews: Using AI to interview departing employees and create a "virtual clone" of their knowledge for successors.	ChatGPT, Gemini
Playbook Activation	Coaching Sellers	Interactive chatbots: Deploying custom GPTs or chatbots that allow sellers to query the playbook for specific advice.	Custom GPTs, PlaybookBuilder.ai, Waybook, Flight
	Real-Time Guidance	Just-in-time surfacing: Analyzing CRM context to push relevant playbook snippets to sellers during their workflow.	Highspot, Seismic, Spekit
	Identifying Gaps	Usage analysis: Analyzing call transcripts to see which "plays" are actually used and identifying successful deviations.	Gong, Chorus.ai
Playbook Optimization	Updating Content	Autonomous evolution: Agents that monitor competitor news and win/loss data to automatically generate new battle cards.	Beam.ai (Custom Workflows)

AI FOR BOARD COMMUNICATION AND ALIGNMENT

The CRO's job isn't just to manage a great sales organization that hits its numbers—they also need to communicate the plan to their board, and their progress against it.

Even in the best of times, sales leaders can be overwhelmed with requests for information from their boards, and when things are going poorly, this can devolve into an unending demand for more and more information. AI provides the opportunity to rethink and reinvent this relationship, making both the executive and the board happier.

AUTOMATING BASIC BOARD REPORTING

Working in PE-backed companies, I've learned that there's a cadence of weekly, monthly, and quarterly communications with my boards that govern our relationship—and my ability to deliver a clear, data-backed narrative is crucial.

Yet for many operators, this process can be a never-ending, manual exercise in data assembly and slide writing, which takes time away from strategic thinking and work in the business.

AI tools offer a path to reclaim that time and shift the focus from a backward-looking summary of what happened to a forward-looking, strategic conversation.

Level 1: Foundational

The foundational level of AI use in board relationships focuses on the high-effort, low-value tasks of board reporting. Whether it's creating a weekly "flash report" of performance, a monthly bookings summary, or a quarterly review, AI is great for automating the repetitive, nonstrategic work of collecting CRM and other data into board-ready slides.

Once the data is collected, AI can also be used to write a great deal of the qualitative narrative to explain it. By feeding a generative AI tool key reports, it can develop an executive summary as a jumping-off point for telling your own narrative—changing your task from writing the story to editing a well-started draft.

Tools like **Polymer Search** and **Domo** include native AI tools to suggest relevant charts for a live, interactive dashboard that mirrors your existing standard reports—and tools like **Vengage, Decktopus,** or **Presentations.ai** might prompt you to draft an insightful executive summary of what the data says about your business.

Level 2: Advanced

Beyond reporting the news with attractive slides, platforms like **Petavue** and **Domo** imagine board reports to be a conversational interface, one that board members can interrogate through a chat window to ask natural language questions about the data they summarize.

A board member might ask the tool to "model the impact on ARR and profitability if we accelerate the hire of three senior account managers, bringing them on board in June instead of November." The system would then pull data from all relevant systems and generate an answer with a chart, graph, or summary that the Board can immediately discuss taking action on.

In such cases, the AI tool is not replacing the judgment of the CRO to lead the business effectively, but it's rapidly accelerating their ability to explore many alternatives and elevate their conversation to a strategic level of "What can we do" vs. "What is happening in the business today."

If implemented, you'll want to ensure that each model's scenario can be traced back to verifiable CRM or ERP data—ensuring the board has the information needed to proceed with the due care mandated for each of their decisions.

As a former CRO, I know this capability has the potential to invite my board members—who already love "being in my business"—to get even more involved in day-to-day operations. That's not great for any of us, though, as their function is an oversight—not an operational— one. When considering using AI to create more interactivity in board conversations, you'll want to think carefully about the cultural, operational, and even legal ramifications of inviting this higher level of involvement.

Level 3: AI-Enabled

At the end of board meetings, there are a number of AI tools that can help summarize decisions, assign tasks for action, and otherwise support board governance processes. As we think about what fully AI-enabled board communications might look like, we can imagine that functionality from vendors like **Diligent**, **Board Intelligence**, or **Workiva** might evolve to include AI agents that proactively drive the action items forward, engaging with relevant stakeholders until all actions have been taken.

Remembering that board meeting minutes fill a specific legal function— serving as the primary evidence that they have fulfilled their fiduciary duties—the person who writes meeting minutes walks a fine line to make them detailed enough to show that the board knew what they were doing, but vague enough to avoid creating discoverable evidence of wrongdoing. This is why most general counsels avoid verbatim transcripts or recordings of board meetings.

Case Study: Reliable Board Reporting for $30/Month

The Challenge

A fast-growing provider in a specialized healthcare niche faced a resource gap common in early-stage organizations. While the team was managing enterprise-sized deals, the operational monitoring and reporting processes were largely manual.

- **Absence of revenue operations (RevOps):** The organization lacked a dedicated team to collect, clean, or interpret data from the existing technology stack.

- **Extreme data fragmentation:** The annual planning process was manual, requiring the manual reconciliation of **23 different spreadsheets** over several weeks.

- **Historical blind spots:** Without the tools to analyze historical performance, leadership relied on "gut feel" rather than scientific understanding of seasonality and other trends.

The Solution: AI-driven "Rev Ops"

The head of sales developed an AI agent to partner with him as a surrogate RevOps analyst.

- **Iterative AI "onboarding":** Treating the AI agent as a new hire rather than a software tool, the leader used **80 to 100 prompts** to calibrate the agent's understanding of the business.

- **Deep pattern recognition:** Once calibrated, the agent analyzed four years of CRM data to identify hidden trends. This included uncovering specific seasonal windows when RFP volume spiked and win rates fluctuated—trends which were previously invisible to the human team.

- **Automated scenario modeling:** The agent generated three distinct forecast models (moderate, aggressive, and conservative) based on historical revenue per seller and deal velocity.

> - **Operationalized weekly reporting:** The system transitioned into an execution partner. Every Monday morning, the agent proactively generates a seller-by-seller pipeline report, performing "sanity checks" on deal probabilities and highlighting stalled opportunities that the leader uses to prioritize his day.
>
> **The ROI**
>
> - **Scientific validation:** The AI-generated annual plan was approved "almost instantly" by the board of directors, who explicitly noted the newfound level of scientific rigor in the organization's projections.
>
> - **Extreme labor arbitrage:** The organization successfully replicated the output of a full-time RevOps Analyst for the cost of a standard **$30-per-month** subscription.
>
> - **Forecast precision:** The organization established a clear, data-backed path to achieving **5–10% forecast accuracy** for the fiscal year.

A scenario in which a written record has been developed that suggests the company was given a specific directive to take an action that was never completed opens serious legal liability. Evidence that your board made an informed decision but failed to provide reasonable oversight to ensure that it was put into action is a serious failure of governance that can have dramatic consequences—and your team will want to think carefully about these issues when determining how deeply to integrate AI into these processes.

PREPARING FOR INVESTMENTS, M&A, OR EXITS

With a career in PE-backed companies, I know that "the exit" is a key destination that my boards and executive colleagues are always keeping an eye on. When the time comes to begin this process, it can feel like a second full-time job to prepare for and execute all of the steps involved in the transaction.

It's also an important one—the ability to strategically position the business to the right buyers with speed and precision can drive a multimillion-dollar difference in final valuation, which directly impacts the financial outcome for everyone involved. AI is emerging as a critical tool for creating a smoother, faster, and more valuable exit.

Level 1: Foundational

To begin an exit process, a confidential information memorandum (CIM) is written, which serves as the marketing brochure for the company. It's often over 100 pages long and includes details about product and market positioning, financial reports, and executive bios. Today, the CIM creation process is extremely manual and takes a lot of time and effort from the operating team and investment backers who synthesize data from many sources into a single, coherent, and exciting story for potential investors.

Recently, a category of AI platforms has been built specifically to help create deal documents, ingesting financial statements, board decks, product documents, and market research reports to produce a strong first draft of the CIM's core sections.

Level 2: Advanced

With platforms like **Deliverables.ai** and **V7 Go**, AI agents can be deployed to evolve the CIM by scanning news articles and other public data, finding relevant case law, or finding comps to build valuations to include in the positioning.

ENGAGING WITH BUYERS

For years, these transactions have been supported by virtual deal rooms—secure, online repositories of documents and discussions between the company and its potential buyers. Yet AI has the potential to transform how these rooms work—shifting them from simply being information portals to insight providers for the people involved in marketing a business.

Level 2: Advanced

First, AI-powered deal rooms can speed the process of organizing information for presentation. Tools like **Datasite** or **Intralinks** might scan through the thousands of pages of documentation to identify and suggest redactions for personally identifiable information or other sensitive material before sharing with potential bidders—a manual task that otherwise might have taken hundreds of hours of junior lawyers' and analysts' time.

At the same time, tools like **Ansarada** and **DealRoom** might also start to identify trends in which bidders are engaging with which materials, and the amount of time spent on them.

An AI tool may surface, for example, that one bidder has spent 15 hours in the data room, with 85% of their time focused on financial statements and key customer contracts, while another bidder logged in for five minutes, read the management bios, and never returned again. Such insights might suggest which meetings the management team should spend a lot of time preparing for and which are lower priorities to engage with.

Level 3: AI-Enabled

AI tools also have the potential to turn the deal room on its head—changing from one where a company provides information about itself to others to one where the company first learns about itself.

In a "self-diligence" model, an organization might first use tools like **V7 Go** or **DealRoom** to run a full analysis of its own draft data room before launching the sales process. The AI tools might scan every customer contract for problematic clauses or suggest revenue synergies with a range of potential strategic buyers so the organization can take action to bolster key features of its business before going to market.

In each of these use cases, your governance council will want to pay particular attention to data security (protecting these most highly confidential documents) and disclosures to others about what is being tracked and monitored through AI.

IN SUM

For the CRO, the board relationship is often one defined by a tension between the need for transparent communication and the burden of manual reporting. Often, the volume of requests and breadth of topics discussed means sales leaders spend weeks assembling backward-looking data into slides, leaving little time to actually analyze the strategic implications of what they're reporting.

AI has the potential to fundamentally reshape this dynamic by creating faster, more accurate, and predictive reporting that the CRO can use to drive alignment on where the business goes next.

Use this summary table to organize your thinking about the application of AI for board-related processes.

Process Stage	Specific Task	AI Application	Example Vendors/ Products
Board Reporting	Automating Updates	Flash reports & drafts: Automating the collection of CRM data into decks and using Generative AI to draft executive summaries.	Polymer Search, Domo, Vengage, Decktopus, Presentations.ai
	Scenario Planning	Conversational analytics: Allowing board members to query data via chat to model "what-if" scenarios (e.g., hiring impact on ARR).	Petavue, Domo
Board Governance	Action Tracking	Agentic follow-up: Agents that summarize meetings, assign tasks, and chase stakeholders for completion.	Diligent, Board Intelligence, Workiva
M&A Preparation	Asset Creation	Drafting the CIM: Ingesting financial and product documents to generate the first draft of the confidential information memorandum.	Deliverables.ai, V7 Go

Process Stage	Specific Task	AI Application	Example Vendors/ Products
M&A Execution	Data Room Management	Automated redaction: Scanning thousands of documents to identify and redact sensitive/PII data instantly.	Datasite, Intralinks
	Buyer Intelligence	Bidder engagement tracking: Analyzing time-spent metrics in the VDR to identify which buyers are serious and what they value.	Ansarada, DealRoom
M&A Strategy	Risk Mitigation	Self-diligence: Proactively scanning your own contracts and data room to identify risks or synergy opportunities before going to market.	V7 Go, DealRoom

LEGAL AND ETHICAL CONSIDERATIONS FOR AI IN SALES

As AI tools move from a novelty to a necessity for sales organizations, they attract increased security. As we've seen with previous new technologies, the legal landscape is evolving at different speeds across different geographies.

When AI use cases move from simple task automation use cases like email scheduling to agentic uses (where AI tools operate as "digital workers" that observe, reason, and execute complex workflows with minimal human oversight), regulatory scrutiny is likely to increase—and businesses should expect that the laws governing their use of AI tools will remain in flux for the foreseeable future before universal standards emerge.

In the meantime, organizations would be well served by applying rigorous ethical examinations to their practices, as the gap between what is legal and what is ethical is rapidly closing in many applications—and legal mandates are often implemented in response to prior ethical breaches.

THE CURRENT LEGAL LANDSCAPE

While the legal landscape continues to evolve, this chapter serves as a guide to key regulations that impact AI in sales at the time of this writing.

THE EU AI ACT

For organizations that operate with a global footprint—or those who believe that the US will follow Europe's lead—the European Union's Artificial Intelligence Act presents a clear compliance benchmark. It went into effect on August 1, 2024, with a series of rules phasing in through August 2027.

The Act doesn't just apply to European companies, however. It also regulates any organizations that put AI tools to use within the European Union and—importantly—organizations in third countries (such as the US) if the output from their systems is used in the EU. This means, for example, that a US-based sales team that uses the AI features of its lead generation tools to engage with European prospects is also subject to the EU AI Act.

Emotional Recognition

In February 2025, the AI Act prohibited eight practices considered threats to the safety, livelihoods, and rights of people, including using AI tools for manipulation, deception, and exploitation of vulnerabilities.

Notably, it also prohibited the use of AI tools to infer the emotions of people in workplaces and educational settings, except for medical or safety reasons. This has clear implications for the use of AI tools as "sales coaches," which have historically used "sentiment analysis" to monitor conversations that sellers have with prospects.

If such use cases are inferring a European seller's emotional state (grading them on their enthusiasm, empathy, or aggression, for example), the use case may run afoul of the law. At the same time, the European Commission also identifies a critical distinction—while the Act prohibits inferring the emotions of a *worker*, the prohibition may not apply to inferring the emotions of a *customer* (where, for example, voice analytics in a call center may identify angry customers for routing decisions)—provided that the system doesn't manipulate the customer's decision-making ability.

This distinction is nuanced and may be interpreted differently by different authorities, so it is an area to watch as it evolves.

High Risk Decisions

In August 2026 and 2027, the Act calls for new obligations on "high-risk AI systems" which may require special attention in the sales context.

First, AI tools that are used to evaluate the creditworthiness or credit score of natural persons are considered "high risk." If organizations are using automated credit approval workflows or autonomously determining payment terms for customers based on algorithmic risk assessments, the Act requires them to also maintain detailed technical documentation and ensure that the data used to train their models is free of discriminatory bias.

Similarly, using AI to recruit sales team members (for resume screening or scoring, for example), or for algorithmically managing tasks (like determining which sellers receive which leads as a result of performance assessments) also triggers these obligations.

Chatbot Transparency

The Act also implements transparency requirements in August 2026 that require humans to be made aware that they're interacting with AI tools like chatbots, so they can make informed decisions about their engagement. AI-generated content also needs to be clearly and visibly labeled as such.

For sales context, this means that sales chatbots, automated BDRs, or customer service agents need to be clearly identified as AI tools—where previously a human photo and name may have led people to believe they were engaging with a "live" representative.

GENERAL DATA PROTECTION REGULATION

While the EU AI Act focuses on the safety and transparency of the technology itself, the General Data Protection Regulation (GDPR) remains the primary law governing the personal data consumed by those tools. For sales organizations, AI doesn't change the rules of GDPR, but it significantly raises the stakes of compliance, with a few key issues to focus on.

"Secondary Use" Challenges

AI solutions are often trained on large data sets, but GDPR requires that data be collected for "specified, explicit, and legitimate purposes." This means, for example, that if a company is using its customers' financial information for the sole purpose of delivering financial services to them, and the vendor then uses the same data to train an AI tool to determine seasonality in the markets they serve, they are engaging in an unauthorized, secondary use.

The Right to Be Forgotten

Under Article 17, GDPR gives your customers and prospects the right to demand that you delete their data. While it is straightforward to delete email messages or CRM data, it is less clear how to remove the influence that person's data had on the complex machine learning model that powers your AI tools. Consider a situation in which a customer raises a unique objection in the sales process, and AI-based tools continue to train sellers on how to handle the objection even after the customer's data has been removed (and no other prospect has surfaced the same concern). Resolving these complex technical questions remains a point of contention for lawyers and regulators.

Right to Explanation

GDPR Article 22 specifies that people should "not be subject to a decision based solely on automated processing, including profiling," that results in legal or similarly significant effects.[5] If your AI tool independently offers unique pricing to a specific customer or disqualifies

---

[5] "Art. 22 GDPR—Automated Individual Decision-Making, Including Profiling," General Data Protection Regulation (GDPR), July 26, 2018, https://gdpr-info.eu/art-22-gdpr/.

a job applicant from consideration, you must be able to explain the underlying logic driving these decisions.

THE US FEDERAL TRADE COMMISSION ACT

While the United States does not have a similarly targeted, sweeping act specifically built for AI use cases, the Federal Trade Commission Act of 1914 has increasingly been brought to bear in AI contexts—especially Section 5, which prohibits "unfair or deceptive acts or practices."

In September 2024, the FTC announced the launch of "Operation AI Comply," which targets misuse of AI to defraud consumers.

A specific rule that took effect in October 2024 bans businesses from creating or selling fake reviews or testimonials that are represented as being from someone who does not exist—like AI-generated fake reviews or testimonials.

Businesses are also prohibited from selling or buying "fake indicators of social media influence" like followers or views that are generated by a bot.

THE US FEDERAL COMMUNICATIONS COMMISSION AND THE TELEPHONE CONSUMER PROTECTION ACT

For lead generation processes, the US FCC implemented a new consent rule in January 2025 that requires prior written consent for each individual seller who makes robocalls. Previously, a lead generation website might obtain consumer consent with a single checkbox stating "I agree to be contacted by this company and its marketing partners," and then sell the data to multiple "partners" who could bombard them with calls about completely unrelated products.

Under the new consent rule, each partner must obtain its own consent.

At the same time, the FCC issued a Declaratory Ruling confirming that AI tools that generate human voices fall under the Telephone

Consumer Protection Act's restrictions on artificial or prerecorded voice calls. Sales calls that use AI bots that are "interactive" or generate conversation in real-time to participate in a call require the same prior express written consent as a traditional robocall that was prerecorded.

Additionally, proposed rules would require callers using AI-generated voices to clearly disclose at the start of the call that it is an AI bot, so keep watching for a definitive action here if incorporating it into your own process.

THE US DEPARTMENT OF JUSTICE ANTITRUST POSITION

In 2024 and 2025, the DOJ and multiple state attorneys general pursued a property management software company for what they alleged to be an "unlawful scheme to decrease competition."

At issue was a process in which the software allowed landlords of competing properties to share private, competitively sensitive pricing data with the system's algorithm, which then aggregated their data and recommended pricing to all users. The DOJ argued that this constituted an algorithmic version of illegal price-fixing coordination.

In November 2025, the software provider agreed to a settlement that included a few conditions—including a prohibition on using non-public competitor data to train its pricing models (instead relying only on public data or user-specific private data for pricing suggestions).

The settlement also restricts the granularity of pricing information that can be provided—preventing precise coordination by allowing data to only be aggregated at a state-wide level, rather than providing neighborhood-specific insights.

To the extent your sales organization is using AI for pricing optimization, this case (U.S. and Plaintiff States v. RealPage Inc.) may provide a precedent on AI-driven pricing optimization tools that ingest non-public data from competitors, scrape private data, or pool user data across accounts.

THE US COPYRIGHT OFFICE

As generative AI tools are increasingly used to create sales materials (text, video, and images), questions also arise about who owns the output and whose existing copyrights might be infringed upon in the process.

In January 2025, the USCO released "Part 2" of its artificial intelligence report, stating that when a user of an AI tool writes a prompt to create these materials, they do not own the copyright of the produced assets if there is no additional human modification to the outputs.

At the same time, questions have been raised about the data used to train the AI models—particularly whether using copyrighted materials constitutes permitted "fair use," especially when the models produce material that competes with the original works it was trained on.

There is additional legal attention being paid to ownership and usage of data generated by "web scraping" activities, which may be particularly relevant for sales use cases that generate lead lists from online sources.

Precedent on "Autonomous Agent" liability

As organizations move into "agentic AI use cases" in which AI tools can make decisions and execute transactions without human intervention, contract and employment law is increasingly looking to assign blame when errors are made. A few cases in particular have undermined arguments around AI being a "black box" whose decision-making process is not understood as a defense to various accusations.

In 2022, the DOJ announced it had obtained a settlement agreement resolving allegations that Meta engaged in discriminatory advertising in violation of the Fair Housing Act. The complaint alleged that Meta used algorithms to determine which Facebook users received housing ads, and that those algorithms relied in part on characteristics protected under the FHA (using race, color, religion, sex, disability, familial status, and national origin to create "lookalike" or "special ad" audiences who would be shown ads for particular housing options).

In 2022, the Consumer Financial Protection Bureau offered guidance stating that companies that use "complex algorithms" to make lending decisions are nevertheless required to comply with the Equal Credit Opportunity Act to explain to credit applicants the specific reasons they were declined credit.

To comply, the creditor needs to understand what sources of information were used to make the credit decision, and how those sources were used to arrive at the ultimate decision, which would be difficult to defend if the lending decision is made in a "black box" of AI tools that don't offer design transparency.

In 2024, an issue arose in Moffat v. Air Canada when an airline passenger asked the airline's chatbot about bereavement fares. The bot hallucinated a response that the customer should purchase a full-fare ticket and then seek reimbursement for a bereavement discount at a later date. The passenger relied on the bot's advice (which contradicted the airline's official policy page), and sued after being denied the discount.

Air Canada argued that the chatbot was a separate legal entity, and the passenger should have verified the information against the official, correct statement of policies online—but a resolution tribunal rejected this defense, ruling that the chatbot is part of the company's website, and therefore the company is responsible for the accuracy of the information it provides.

The tribunal found that the airline was liable for negligent misrepresentation in this instance. And while this decision came from the British Columbia Civil Resolution Tribunal—and not a court decision—companies that use AI agents that might promise a discount, a delivery date, or a specific contractual term may still find that it suggests they are legally bound to honor the bot's promise.

2025 potentially provided a precedent for algorithmic bias in hiring decisions in Mobley v. Workday. In this matter, Derek Mobley alleged that Workday's AI-based applicant screening tools violated Title VII protections by systematically rejecting his applications based on considerations of age, race, and disability.

In their defense, Workday argued that it was just a software vendor—not the employer—but the judge allowed the case to proceed on the theory that Workday was acting as an "agent" of the employer because it had been delegated the task of screening job applicants.

In May 2025, the court granted preliminary certification for a nationwide collective application—which might set a precedent for AI tools used in hiring decisions to be considered "agents" of the hiring organization who might have direct liability in employment discrimination claims—particularly if the class action suit is successful.

A PATCHWORK OF LOCALE-SPECIFIC LEGISLATION

Across the US, various states have implemented their own AI–related laws, which may have precedent for sales organizations.

THE ILLINOIS BIOMETRIC INFORMATION PRIVACY ACT (BIPA)

One of the most strictly enforced biometric privacy laws in the US is found in Illinois, which identifies six biometric identifiers that can be used to identify an individual: fingerprints, voiceprints, retina scans, iris scans, scans of hand geometry, and scans of face geometry.

Sales organizations that use voice data to identify a customer may want to verify that they're complying with the written consent requirements of this law before collecting the "voiceprint."

Retailers who offer AI-powered "virtual try on" tools for makeup, jewelry, glasses, or other products that interact with facial or hand geometry will also want to pay particular attention to this state's legislation.

THE ENSURING LIKENESS VOICE AND IMAGE SECURITY ACT (TENNESSEE'S ELVIS ACT)

In 2024, Tennessee passed a law that makes it illegal to use AI to simulate an individual's voice or likeness for commercial purposes without their consent—and similar name, image, and likeness laws have been passed in other states.

Sales and marketing teams that use AI avatars or AI-generated marketing materials must ensure that they have explicit releases from the voice actors, actors, or models whose data was used to train the generating tool's capabilities.

CALIFORNIA'S BOT ACT

This act requires that any bot used to incentivize a purchase must disclose its identity and answer questions about its identity truthfully.

UTAH'S AI POLICY ACT

Utah's act introduces a reactive disclosure for AI in general commerce—so that it does not need to declare its identity up front, but must respond truthfully if a customer asks about its identity. Proactive disclosures are required for regulated occupations such as doctors, nurses, veterinarians, accountants, and others.

CALIFORNIA'S CONSUMER PRIVACY ACT (CCPA)

Expansions to this act provide rights to opt out of automated decision-making technologies that profile consumers for decisions around pricing or service access.

COLORADO'S AI ACT

Colorado's AI Act imposes a "duty of care" on developers and users of high-risk AI, so that if an AI tool is used for a consequential decision (like approving financing terms in a B2B deal), the company must have a documented risk management program in place.

Like the Federal Equal Credit Opportunity Act, the Colorado AI Act provides a state-level requirement to notify consumers of the principal reasons adverse decisions were made about them, which might include the degree to which AI systems contributed to the decision, the type of data used to make the decision, and the source of that data. Consumers also need to be provided the opportunity to correct any incorrect personal data that factored into the decision and be offered an opportunity to appeal any adverse decision with human review.

NEW YORK CITY'S LOCAL LAW 114

Established in 2021, this law prohibits employers and employment agencies from using "automated employment decision tools" unless the tool has been subject to a bias audit within one year of its use, information about the audit is made publicly available, and certain notices have been provided to employees and job candidates.

OVERARCHING LEGAL TRENDS

A quick review of case law suggests that AI is rapidly becoming heavily regulated in business contexts, and a few key themes are emerging from legal activity. Some takeaways for sales professionals:

1. **Transparency is of utmost importance.** Whether it's disclosing that a user is interacting with a bot, complying with the FCC's robocall rules, or working under the confines of the EU AI Act, transparency is a recurring theme. AI agents should be clearly labeled, and people should know when AI is used in decision-making.

2. **Data sourcing is critical.** Whether you're training an LLM on copywritten materials, scraping the web for lead lists, or ensuring that you have customer consent to record their conversations for different purposes, you'll want to be thoughtful about how and where you collect the data that drives AI.

3. **Liability cannot be outsourced.** When AI agents interact on behalf of your organization, you cannot disclaim responsibility for the decisions they make. Saying "I don't understand how it did that" is not a defensible excuse for violating promises made on your behalf.

4. **Personal information is personal.** Whether it's biometric data in Illinois or emotional assessments of EU workers, the use of AI to process highly personal information is one to be weighed carefully.

Complying with emerging regulations is essential for risk mitigation—but it only represents the floor for the responsible adoption of AI tools—not the ceiling. Often, legal requirements are put in place as a reaction to harms that have already been done. That's why sustainable AI initiatives will be informed not just by what is legally permissible, but also by what is strategically and morally sound.

ETHICAL TOPICS FOR AI IN SALES

Sales have always been driven by interpersonal trust—between sellers and customers, between managers and their teams, and between leaders and their investors. But when we introduce AI tools as intermediaries in these relationships, we need to think carefully about whether we are using these tools to *fake* a human connection or to *enable* it.

When tools are used to surface insights that make the seller more relevant, the conversation more targeted, or the resulting relationship stronger, they add value. But when tools are used to trick prospects into engaging with someone they believe is an empathetic human—only to later realize they were deceived by a well-scripted bot—the relationship erodes. When the scripting lies, discriminates, or introduces unfair advantages to the process, the relationship completely falls apart.

That's why, when we're deploying new and exciting AI tools, ethics is more than just a slide in an annual compliance training certification; it is the compass for building strong sales teams. And there are a number of important pitfalls we want to watch out for that could undermine our best efforts.

UNINTENTIONAL BIAS: WHEN TRAINING DATA DISCRIMINATES

In August 2025, Arshon Harper filed a class action complaint against Sirius Radio, asserting that the AI tool used to screen and analyze resumes of applicants resulted in racial discrimination against him and other African American applicants by using data points like educational institutions, employment history, and zip codes as proxies for race—rejecting him from approximately 150 positions for which he was allegedly qualified.

The argument suggests that Sirius's AI tools learned from hidden biases inherent in their training data, echoing an experience Amazon had years previously. There, tools purportedly observed that most successful applicants were men (reflecting the fact that most applications came from men, who dominate the tech industry), and therefore penalized resumes that included credentials like "women's chess club captain" or graduates of all-women's colleges, until the engine was changed and then ultimately the project was scrapped.

While both of these examples suggest discrimination based on legally prohibited considerations, a similar issue may arise when AI tools make scoring decisions on non-protected, but similarly flawed, data points.

Consider a lead scoring system that evaluates a lead's propensity to buy with a "black box" algorithm that will either enroll them in a high-touch sales engagement or a low-touch nurture sequence. If the tool were trained on conversation data from years when a company had little sales presence—but now is operating with a wider geographical footprint—it may erroneously have learned that prospects from previously underserved postal codes are unlikely to convert. This "learning" artificially lowers the organization's service obtainable market, or incorrectly introduces discrimination into the customers they'll service.

THE PANOPTICON: VIOLATING PRIVACY AND SURVEILLANCE EXPECTATIONS

My undergraduate philosophy degree introduced me to the idea of the "panopticon"—a type of prison design invented by Jeremy Bentham that features a central tower surrounded by cells whose inhabitants can't tell when they're being watched. Knowing that guards can see into any cell at any time, the uncertainty and feeling of constant surveillance drive prisoners to behave as if they are always observed, internalizing a sense of self-discipline.

As AI tools increasingly record and transcribe every digital call and every email is scrutinized for various indicators of adherence to the sales playbook, sales teams may start behaving as if they're working in a digital panopticon.

Knowing that every pause, tone shift, or delay in responding to a customer email may flag the seller for follow-up training or coaching, AI tools may risk creating a performative environment where sellers "act" for the algorithm on their calls, rather than truly connecting with their clients.

Transparency and consent are also critical considerations for the ethical use of AI. While customers and prospects are increasingly familiar with hearing their call "may be recorded for quality assurance purposes," they may believe that it simply means the seller's manager may listen to the call at some point in the future. They're unlikely to truly understand that their conversation might be used to train a third-party vendor's voice cloning algorithm, or that they're being turned into "mock prospect avatars" for sellers to train with at a later date. They also may not realize that sentiment analysis is assessing their propensity to buy—or that tools are being used to identify key emotional triggers that might be exploited to manipulate that propensity in the future.

THE GTM AI GOVERNANCE COUNCIL

To navigate concerns like these—and more—tech leaders like Salesforce, Microsoft, and OneTrust have offered examples of ways to implement an AI governance council to serve as an internal regulatory body for the users of AI in your organization. They help manage the critical balance between the "move fast and break things" instinct of sales organizations and the "manage risk at all costs" impulses of legal teams.

While an AI governance council should likely be in place for the *entire* company, this book's recommendations focus on the specific needs of the professional sales organization.

THE COUNCIL'S MISSION

That's why our council may align around a mission statement like "To accelerate the adoption of high-impact AI tools within the go-to-market organization while strictly mitigating legal, reputational, and ethical risks, the AI governance council serves not as a roadblock to innovation, but as its guardrails."

GOVERNANCE COUNCIL MEMBERSHIP

The council's membership might include the following people:

- Chief revenue officer: acts as chair and owns the business outcome of the council's work

- Chief legal officer/or compliance officer owns issues regarding adherence to regulations such as the EU AI Act, GDPR, and others
- Chief information security officer: owns data privacy and vendor security issues
- Chief HR officer/inclusion leader: owns the impact on hiring bias, talent assessment, and employee surveillance
- RevOps leader: owns the tactical implementation and management of vendor relationships

KEY QUESTIONS FOR THE GOVERNANCE COUNCIL

As they go about their work, the council will engage with a variety of questions that have important implications for the organization. These include:

- **Data Provenance Questions**. Because using tools that are trained on scraped, non-consensual data can expose the company to IP lawsuits and regulatory fines, the council will want to ask questions such as "What data was this model trained on?" "Do we have the legal right to use it?" "Does the vendor have the legal right to sell it?"
- **Bias Questions**: Recognizing that a model may have been trained on data that was unintentionally biased—and therefore creates disparate impacts for different groups of people—the council might ask "Have we tested this AI tool's performance specifically against protected subgroups of people (specifically race, age, gender, and sexual orientation) to ensure the false positive/negative rates are equal across all populations?"
- **Explainability Question**: Because regulations increasingly conclude that if you can't explain the "black box" decision-making technology, you can't use it, the council should ask, "If our AI tool rejects a job candidate, deprioritizes a customer lead,

or denies a credit application, can we explain to them exactly why this happened?"

- **Liability Question**: If this AI agent hallucinates a false promise or a libelous statement, will the vendor or us be liable? Most SaaS contracts (and therefore most contracts you'll see for vendors of your AI tools) attempt to shift all liability to the end user of their software—so the council will want to be sure they've negotiated indemnification clauses and insurance coverage for AI errors.

- **Displacement Questions:** If AI tools are now "the lowest cost resource" that some work tasks can be deployed to, they are fundamentally changing the nature of someone's job. The council should ask, "Are we using AI to assist our sellers or to replace them?" "If it's displacement, do we have a reskilling plan?" "If it's complete elimination, have we considered how we will communicate, maintain morale, and avoid alienating employees in jobs we want to keep?"

- **The "Front Page" Question:** If our use of this technology, or a transcript of this AI tool's conversation with a customer, were published on the front page of a key newspaper, would we be embarrassed? What reputational damage would we sustain? Is it outweighed by the efficiency gains we get from using this tool?

GOVERNANCE COUNCIL RULES

While some of these conversations can be highly intellectual, the council is not just a thought leader on vague AI topics for their organization—they also need to be empowered to enforce practical, tactical rules for the use of AI. Some rules and enforcement actions they might consider include:

- **The Transparency Mandate:** Any interaction involving an AI agent (a chatbot, a voice agent, or an automated email system) must disclose its non-human identity immediately. Periodically, the council will engage a mystery shopper to audit email sequences and chatbots to ensure this disclosure is present and clear in all communications.

- **"Human in the Loop" Requirements:** No high-stakes decision—including hiring offers and rejections, contract creations, and financial commitments—can be finalized by AI alone. A human must review and sign off after understanding the key inputs to the decision. The council will ensure that any sales tools making these decisions will have a manual, human approval step embedded in their workflow.

- **Zero Private Data in Public LLMs:** No confidential customer information, pricing strategy, personally identifying information, confidential information, protected IP, or trade secrets may be entered into a public, non-enterprise LLM (like the free version of ChatGPT). The council will ensure that IT monitoring systems are in place alongside strict procurement policies that allow only "zero data retention" enterprise licenses for generative AI tools.

- **No Impersonation:** The use of AI voice cloning to mimic specific individuals (the CEO, a key client, or celebrity endorser) for any use will be strictly prohibited without explicit written consent from the voice owner. The council will immediately terminate contracts with vendors or partners found using deepfake technology for unauthorized impersonations in prospecting, endorsement, or any other business purpose.

- **Bias Auditing:** Any AI tool used for decisions about our people—hiring, firing, promotion, territory assignment, or compensation planning—must undergo an annual bias audit to ensure it does not discriminate against protected classes. The council will ensure that these tools are reviewed annually against standards such as NYC Local Law 114 and produce an audit report and an endorsement of continued use for internal purposes.

THE EVOLUTION OF GOVERNANCE

As they undertake their work, the governance council may find they're taking on projects that fall into a few categories of work:

Early-stage work is focused on the basics of legal compliance and simple transparency. Here, projects are undertaken to ensure the bare minimum is done to ensure legal compliance and avoid deception:

- All chatbots and automated agents clearly identify themselves as AI.

- Email signatures are modified to include "AI-assisted" where appropriate.

- Compliance with GDPR and CCPA is maintained. Ensure sales calls are recorded only with the required notification and consent.

- Publish an "acceptable use policy" for AI, prohibiting employees from inputting confidential information into public LLMs and other key policies.

With basic legal protections in place, projects may move into those that support oversight and auditing to ensure fairness, accuracy, and human judgment are maintained:

- Projects are launched to ensure vendors have delivered bias audit certifications as needed, and internal and audit teams are set up to conduct regular fairness audits of hiring and lead-scoring tools.

- Audits are conducted of key business processes to ensure that all high-stakes decisions have a human in the final decision-making role.

- Hallucination management: Projects are launched to refine training data and protect customer-facing agents from making statements that are inaccurate, misleading, or otherwise wrong.

The most sophisticated organizations will also undertake projects that promote ethical AI use as a valuable end in itself:

- Much like the penetration testing that has become commonplace for IT security teams, the organization creates a "red team testing group" to actively try to break their own AI agents—attempting to trick AI bots into offering unauthorized discounts, using offensive language, or otherwise discrediting the organization through vulnerabilities before putting them into production.

- Dynamic consent: Privacy preferences get managed dynamically, so that if a customer opts out of tracking in one system, an AI agent autonomously propagates that request across the entire tech stack.

- Operating principle training: The AI tools are given a defined list of core operating principles (like being honest, harmless, and helpful), which they must use to critique their own work before delivering responses to end users.

WHERE THIS IS ALL HEADING

In late 2022, when ChatGPT made many people aware of AI for the first time ever, simple prompts created awe-inspiring magic tricks. In the ensuing years, what were initially impressive evolutions—writing poems, writing articles, generating images, generating videos—quickly became old hat. And soon, pundits started asking where it was all heading.

In 2023, Sequoia Capital's David Cahn raised what he called "AI's $200B question," noting that tech companies had spent billions on AI infrastructure without a clear path to revenue growth that would justify the investment. By June 2024, he'd updated his question to be "AI's $600B question."

As analysis anticipates global spending on AI to top $3 trillion in the near future, these questions will start to become more important for every company to answer—no longer should we be asking if it's possible for AI to write an email, generate a marketing brochure, or summarize a phone call—we need to think about how we can use these capabilities to move the needle on the bottom line.

At the same time, many professionals are still unsure about what the tools can do for them—at the end of 2025, only 19% of US workers reported using AI at work—while others ask if it will put them out of a job.

We can find guidance on these questions by looking at past periods of rapid technological advancement.

In the late 1990s, when the internet felt like an unproven fad, we saw similar skepticism about the money that was being poured into it—and we did live through an investment bubble that ultimately burst. Yet the technology didn't go away afterward—it became a basic utility that is an intrinsic part of the world, with internet access now as ubiquitous—and important—as electricity and water supplies to modern businesses.

Two hundred years earlier, during the Industrial Revolution that carried the world into the 1800s, machines didn't eliminate the value of fine craftsmanship—they just changed the places where human effort was applied. As repetitive tasks were mechanized, human creativity and oversight became *more* valuable, and wages for these creative workers increased.

While I may not know exactly when AI tools will enter their "utility phase," I do believe we would be wrong to dismiss or ignore them. There will be many missteps made along the way—from hallucinations to biased models—and legislation, ethical guidelines, and strong corporate AI governance councils will help us navigate them.

Ultimately, I'm convinced it will become part of the corporate DNA of every future organization, and the bar will be raised—even for entry-level professionals—to shift from being data manipulators to value-adding interpreters and strategy-setters.

That's why it's so important for sales professionals to start experimenting with AI today, if they haven't already. In each chapter of this book, we've seen a number of low-risk ways to start experimenting with AI—but the era of "experimentation for experimentation's sake" is soon ending for the sales professional. As custom-built tools are built for organization-wide deployment—and some innovators explore with autonomous agents that can execute extended workflows independently—the role of the sales professional is definitely going to change.

Even as these advances are made, AI tools remain limited as data processors and pattern identifiers. On the surface, that might feel like a simulated personality—but it does not substitute for the deep interpersonal trust-building that's at the core of every complex sale. Skills such as empathy, perspective-taking, group consensus-building, and much more are still only held by living, breathing people.

The word only spins forward, and AI is now a part of it. The best sellers will use it to amplify their humanity. The time has come.

BONUS MATERIALS

Additional materials—including a library of AI prompts and a summary spreadsheet of AI use cases and products described in this book—can be found online at:

jdmillerphd.com/ai-handbook-bonus-materials

bit.ly/AIBookBonus

ACKNOWLEDGMENTS

The insights and frameworks shared in this book are not finished; they are my best current attempt to make sense of a journey that is very much in progress. In 25 years, I've seen many transformational innovations for sellers and our customers. I am deeply grateful to the experts who patiently explained each new advancement to me as it arrived, helping me evolve alongside the technology—from the pioneering days of the early web to the agentic AI landscape we are building today.

I want to extend my deepest gratitude to the AI vendors who took the time to share what they are building and the companies who shared what they are implementing. Your willingness to walk me through your innovations, setbacks, and visions of the future was invaluable.

I am equally thankful for the companies, board colleagues, and executive teams who currently trust me for guidance on these topics. It's a privilege to get firsthand experience with how these mysterious new tools can be applied to solve real business problems. Your candid feedback and shared curiosity keep my perspective grounded in the practical challenges of modern selling.

In bringing this manuscript to life, I am also deeply indebted to the editing, design, and production teams at Catalyst Ink. Your ability to sharpen my voice and provide structure to my words is a testament to the truth that doing work to be proud of requires talented professionals from many disciplines. Thank you for your patience and for the rigor you brought to this project.

Finally, I want to acknowledge the people in my life who provide the "humanity" that anchors this work. While the algorithms and agents this book explores are remarkable, it is my friends and family who truly bring the zest and meaning that make life joyful.

ABOUT THE AUTHOR

JD Miller, PhD, is a go-to-market leader in Private Equity. As an Operating Advisor, he brings decades of experience in multinational tech companies to build high-performing teams and implement growth strategies.

Drawing on his organizational communication research, JD leverages his expertise at the intersection of business, technology, and humanity to strengthen the companies he works with. He is the author of *The CRO's Guide to Winning in Private Equity* and a featured TEDx speaker.

He serves on multiple corporate and nonprofit boards, and his work in empowering underserved communities earned him recognition as one of Chicago's Most Inspiring Individuals.

ALSO BY THIS AUTHOR
THE CRO'S GUIDE TO WINNING IN PRIVATE EQUITY

In the high-stakes world of private equity-backed companies, chief revenue officers face unique challenges and opportunities. *The CRO's Guide to Winning in Private Equity* offers a comprehensive roadmap for sales leaders looking to excel in this dynamic environment.

Drawing from decades of experience, JD Miller provides an insider's perspective on navigating the complexities of PE-backed sales leadership. *This practical guide covers essential topics, including:*

- Crafting data-driven annual plans and sales strategies
- Building and motivating high-performing teams
- Implementing effective compensation structures
- Mastering the art of forecasting and board communication
- Driving collaboration between sales and marketing
- Navigating PE exits and leadership transitions

Miller's insights go beyond theory, offering actionable advice, real-world examples, and proven tactics for sales leadership excellence. *Readers will learn how to:*

- Build annual plans that maximize their chance of succeeding

- Develop a "SMarketing" culture that aligns sales and marketing efforts
- Conduct effective quarterly business reviews and deal clinics
- Advocate for themselves in employment negotiations
- Prepare for and manage successful PE exits

Whether you're a seasoned CRO or an aspiring sales leader, **this book equips you with the tools and knowledge to thrive in the competitive PE landscape.** Miller's guidance will help you drive exceptional results, maximize company value, and advance your career in the process.

GET YOUR COPY

bit.ly/CROsGuide

INDEX

9 7 9 8 8 9 5 7 6 1 9 5 3